french provincial cuisine

french provincial cuisine

Christian Roland Délu

BARRON'S

Introduction

'French Country Cooking' is a book of recipes, but it is also a pictorial guide. All my childhood memories centre round the kitchen, and I have worn out many a wooden spoon preparing meals for friends and acquaintances.

Gastronomy is currently one of the areas in which I exercise my profession as a photographer. Most of the following dishes form part of everyday life in France. I have collected them into a kind of family cook-book. They exemplify the Frenchman's continuing delight in his food and his pleasure in entertaining around his table.

In my capacity as a photographer, I have chosen to illustrate these recipes with my favourite photographs, taken for those publications with which I work. They depict the character and simplicity of the dishes that I like to serve at my own table.

Christian Roland Délu

Contents

1
Entrées

Terrine de volaille
Chicken pâté

For 6 to 8 servings:

- 1.2 kg (2 lb 9 oz) chicken
- 500 g (1 lb 2 oz) sausage meat with herbs
- 170 g (6 oz) larding bacon
- salt, pepper
- 3 teaspoons brandy

Bone the chicken and keep the meat from the breast and legs to one side. Mince the remaining meat and the chicken liver and blend with the sausage meat. Season this stuffing with salt and pepper. Add the brandy. Line a 25 cm (10 in) terrine with some of the larding bacon and fill with the stuffing, interspersing with layers of chicken slices and strips of larding bacon. Cover with foil. Put in a bain marie. Cook for 1½-2 hours in a moderate oven Mark 4, 350°F (180°C) and allow to cool.
Serve with salad.
It is important to choose the right sort of bird: the pâté will taste better if made with a good, young chicken or even a free-range chicken.

Suggested wines:

Bourgueil, Chinon, Saint-Emilion

Pâté en croûte au fromage de chèvre - *Poitou*
Goat's cheese pâté in a pastry crust

For 8 servings:

- 600 g (1 lb 5 oz) short pastry
- 6 small (300 g (10 oz) total weight) goat's-milk cheeses
- 150 g (5 oz) Gruyère cheese
- 150 g (5 oz) ham
- 1 clove garlic
- salt, pepper
- ⅓ l (½ pt) milk
- 2 tablespoons flour
- 3 egg yolks
- 50 g (2 oz) butter
- chives

Carefully line a well-buttered 25 cm (10 in) pâté mould with the short pastry, leaving no space for the stuffing to escape. Then prepare a very thick bechamel sauce with the butter, flour and milk. Leave to cool and add the grated Gruyère cheese with the chopped ham, chives and garlic. Season with salt and pepper and fold in the egg yolks. The consistency of the filling should be very stiff.
Place three goat's cheeses in the pâté mould, covering first with the stuffing, then the three remaining cheeses, and finally with the rest of the stuffing. Make a pastry lid with a vent in the centre, and cook in a moderate oven Mark 4, 350°F (180°C) for approximately 1½ hours.
Remove from the oven and allow to cool.
Serve with salad.
Every time I serve this dish to my guests they are greatly surprised to find cheese where they expected meat. For best results, it is essential both that the bechamel sauce be extremely thick and the goat's cheese very dry and strong in taste.

Suggested wines:

Muscadet, Gros Plant

Pâté en croûte
Pâté in a pastry crust

For 8 servings:

- 600 g (1 lb 5 oz) short pastry
- 300 g (11 oz) boneless veal
- 300 g (11 oz) pork
- 100 g (3½ oz) fat bacon
- 150 g (5 oz) pig's liver
- 1 tablespoon parsley
- 1 tablespoon chives
- 4 eggs
- salt, pepper
- 1 teaspoon brandy

Cover the base and sides of a 25 cm (10 in) pâté mould with short pastry seasoned well with pepper. Retain some of the pastry for the lid. Mince the veal and pork and cut the liver and bacon into strips. Add the eggs, salt, pepper, brandy, together with the chopped parsley and chives, to the minced meats.
Spread a layer of this filling over the pastry, and on top place strips of pig's liver and bacon. Repeat this process, ending with a layer of filling, and cover everything with the reserved pastry. Pierce a hole in the centre and decorate the top with pastry shapes. Glaze with egg and cook in a moderate oven Mark 4, 350°F (180°C) for about 1½ hours.
Serve cold with salad.

Suggested wines:

Brouilly, Beaujolais, Bourgueil

Pâté aux herbes
Herb pâté

For 8 to 10 servings:

- 500 g (1 lb 2 oz) sausage meat with herbs
- 500 g (1 lb 2 oz) ham
- 700 g (1 lb 9 oz) boneless veal
- salt, pepper
- 2 bay-leaves
- 1 sprig thyme
- 150 g (5 oz) parsley and chives
- ½ glass brandy or armagnac

Chop the meats with a knife and blend with the sausage meat. Season with salt and pepper. Add brandy or armagnac, chopped parsley, chives, bay-leaves and thyme.
Fill a 25 cm (10 in) terrine with this mixture, cover with foil, place in a bain marie and cook in a moderate oven Mark 4, 350°F (180°C) for 1–1½ hours.
Serve cold with salad and gherkins.
This pâté is easy to make and keeps well. It may be prepared in advance for a picnic.

Suggested wine:

Passe-tout-grain

Canapés aux anchois
Anchovy canapés

For 6 servings:

- 6 thin slices bread
- 8 anchovies in oil
- 1 clove garlic
- 50 g (2 oz) butter
- 3 tomatoes
- 1 stick celery

Cut six slices of bread and toast on both sides. Meanwhile, crush the garlic and anchovies in a mortar. Add the butter and mix well together. Spread the toasted slices of bread with the anchovy paste and garnish with rounds of tomato and some celery stalks with their tops.

Terrine de lièvre
Hare pâté

For 8 servings:

- 1.5 kg (3 lb 4 oz) small hare
- 500 g (1 lb 2 oz) pork meat
- 300 g (11 oz) fat bacon
- 1 small glass brandy
- salt, pepper
- larding bacon
- veal bones
- thyme, bay-leaves
- 1 medium size onion
- 2 cloves
- 1 dessertspoon oil

Bone the hare. Gently brown the hare and veal bones in a casserole dish with the chopped onion. When they are nicely browned, add $\frac{1}{2}$ l (1 pt) of water, thyme, bay-leaves and cloves. Season with salt and pepper. Bring to the boil and reduce by two-thirds over $1\frac{1}{2}$ hours. Meanwhile, mince the pork and fat bacon. Divide the meat from the hare into two parts: large pieces, cut into small strips, and small pieces, minced. Blend the minced meats together. Line a 30 cm (12 in) terrine with the larding bacon and fill with alternate layers of minced meats and strips of hare meat. Season each layer with salt and pepper. Moisten with the brandy and strained bone stock. Cover with larding bacon, put foil over the terrine, place in a bain marie and cook in a moderate oven Mark 4, 350°F (180°C) for about $1\frac{1}{2}$ hours.

Suggested wines:

Red Burgundy, Bonnes-Mares, Richebourg

Pâté de foie
Liver pâté

For 8 servings:

- **200 g (7 oz) fillet of veal**
- **600 g (1 lb 5 oz) pig's liver**
- **200 g (7 oz) fat bacon**
- **4 eggs**
- **2 medium sized onions**
- **parsley**
- **1 dessertspoon brandy**
- **salt, pepper**
- **larding bacon**

Remove the sinews from the pig's liver and mince all the meats. Add the chopped onions and a good handful of chopped parsley. Season with salt and pepper and blend in the brandy and eggs. Line a 30 cm (12 in) terrine with the larding bacon and fill with the mixture. Cover with a slice of larding bacon and cook in a moderate oven for about 2 hours in a bain marie.

Oeufs brouillés aux truffes - *Périgord*
Scrambled eggs with truffles

For 4 servings:

- **8 new-laid eggs**
- **3 dessertspoons double cream**
- **4 truffles**
- **salt, pepper**
- **bread**

Break the eggs into a bowl and blend with the cream. Season with salt and pepper. Add the juice from the truffles. Cook in a saucepan over a very gentle heat. Stir continuously with a wooden spoon to prevent the eggs from setting too quickly. When the eggs have formed a smooth creamy mixture, stop cooking and add the truffles, cut into strips.
Serve immediately on slices of fried bread or toast.
For best results, do not stint on the truffles.
This dish serves as a perfect entrée for a special occasion. It can be varied by adding some ham.

Suggested wines:

Chambertin, Romanée, Médoc, Pomerol

Oeufs en meurette

Eggs in wine sauce

For 6 servings:

– 6 eggs
– ½ l (1 pt) red Burgundy wine
– 1 medium sized onion
– 1 carrot
– 1 leek
– 2 cloves garlic
– 1 sprig thyme, 1-2 bay-leaves
– salt, pepper
– 1 dessertspoon flour
– 50 g (2 oz) butter
– 1 tablespoon vinegar

Put the wine and thinly sliced vegetables into a saucepan. Add salt, pepper, thyme and bay-leaves. Boil for 30 minutes. Remove the thyme and bay-leaves and pass the rest through a vegetable mill. Return to the boil for a further 5 minutes and thicken with a blend of butter kneaded with flour. Poach the eggs in boiling water to which salt and vinegar have been added.
Serve the eggs coated with the sauce.

Suggested wines:

Juliénas, Red Burgundy

Oeufs en gelée

Eggs in aspic jelly

For 6 servings:

– 6 new-laid eggs
– 3 slices ham
– 200 g (7 oz) aspic jelly flavoured with port
– 1 tablespoon vinegar
– 1 tomato
– pickled onions, olives, mushrooms and
   artichoke hearts
– parsley

Melt the jelly in a bowl over a saucepan of boiling water (*bain marie*). Add enough port to the jelly to obtain the desired flavour. Pour a little of this jelly, say ¼ in deep, into six round or oval dariole moulds. Leave to set in the refrigerator.
Meanwhile, boil some salted water with a tablespoon of vinegar. Poach the eggs in this water, using a soup ladle so that the whites do not break up. When they are cooked and rise to the surface, remove with a skimmer. Place on a plate to drain.
At the bottom of each mould, place a sprig of parsley and a thin slice of tomato on top of the hardened jelly. Over this place a piece of ham, also lining the sides of the mould with ham. Put a cooled poached egg into each mould and cover with melted jelly. Allow to cool and when set, serve with the pickled olives, mushrooms, artichoke hearts, and onions.
This excellent dish calls for the use of very fresh eggs since the yolks must stay runny after poaching. This entrée may be prepared in advance.

Tomates farcies au thon
Stuffed tomatoes with tuna

For 6 servings:

– 6 tomatoes
– 50 g (2 oz) butter
– 200 g (7 oz) tuna in oil
– 1 egg
– olives
– salt and pepper
– 1-2 lemons

Cut the tops off the tomatoes and scoop out the centres. Drain well. With a fork, mash the tuna in its oil with the butter to obtain a smooth paste. Add salt to taste. Hard-boil an egg, cool, and then cut into rounds. Fill each tomato with the tuna paste and decorate with slices of egg and olives.
Serve with quarters of lemon as a first course.
To be moist and appetizing, this dish requires tender tomatoes which are very ripe and flavoursome.

Macaronis au gratin
Baked macaroni with cheese

For 6 servings:

– 500 g (1 lb 2 oz) macaroni
– 50 g (2 oz) butter
– 3 slices ham
– 100 g (3½ oz) Gruyère cheese
– 3 dessertspoons double cream
– salt, pepper

Cook the macaroni in plenty of salted boiling water. When cooked, drain. Grate the cheese. Put the macaroni into an ovenproof dish with half the cheese and the ham, cut into squares. Cover with cream and the remaining grated cheese. Dot with knobs of butter. Season with pepper and brown under the grill.

Pipérade - *Pay Basque Béarn*
Scrambled eggs with peppers

For 6 servings:

- **8 new-laid eggs**
- **3 sweet peppers**
- **3 tomatoes**
- **salt, pepper**
- **2 cloves garlic**
- **2 dessertspoons oil**

Prepare the peppers, remove the seeds and poach for 10 minutes in boiling water. Drain and cut into large pieces. Likewise, poach the tomatoes so that their skins come off easily. Put 2 dessertspoons of oil into a frying pan and gently fry the peppers. Add the tomatoes, roughly cut into quarters, and chopped garlic. Season with salt and pepper. Cook for a further 5 minutes and pour the beaten eggs over. Cook over a medium heat. As soon as the omelette is firm enough, fold over like a pancake, finish cooking, and serve very hot.

Suggested wines:

Madiran, Rouge de Cahors or any good red Bordeaux wine

Omelette aux fines herbes
Herb omelette

For 6 servings:

- **10 new-laid eggs**
- **2 dessertspoons double cream**
- **25 g (1 oz) butter**
- **salt, pepper**
- **25 g (1 oz) parsley**
- **25 g (1 oz) chives**

Break the eggs into a bowl. Whisk vigorously with the cream. Season with salt and pepper. Wash and chop the parsley and chives. Add these herbs to the eggs. Heat the butter in a frying pan and pour in the beaten eggs. Cook on a medium flame, pricking the omelette with a fork to let the raw egg run underneath the set portion. Fold the omelette over with a palette knife and serve immediately. A good omelette should be served in a semi-liquid state. The chives may be replaced by tarragon.

Omelette aux girolles
Chanterelle omelette

For 6 servings:

- 10 new-laid eggs
- 200 g (8 oz) chanterelle mushrooms
  (tinned if not in season)
- 100 g (3½ oz) smoked bacon
- parsley
- salt, pepper
- 25 g (1 oz) butter

Wash and peel the chanterelles, and drain well. Chop the bacon into small pieces. Gently fry the bacon in a frying pan with a little butter. When the bacon begins to brown, add the chanterelles and cook for 15 minutes. Meanwhile, break the eggs into a bowl, add salt, pepper and chopped parsley, and beat. When the chanterelles are cooked, pour the beaten eggs into a separate pan and cook on a medium flame. Half-way through cooking, pour in the chanterelle mushrooms. Finish cooking the omelette and fold in half with a palette knife and serve immediately.

Omelette a l'oseille
Sorrel omelette

For 6 servings:

- 10 eggs
- 15 sorrel leaves
  (spinach leaves can be used)
- salt, pepper
- 25 g (1 oz) butter

Break the eggs into a bowl, add salt and pepper, and beat well. Wash the sorrel, remove the thick part of the stems and roughly chop. Heat the butter in a large frying pan and briskly fry the sorrel for 5 minutes. Pour the beaten eggs over and cook on a medium flame. Fold in half and serve immediately. The first time that the author tried this omelette it was for a mid-morning snack on a farm in the Poitou region. It was served with a big slice of thickly buttered bread, followed by goat's-milk cheese, eaten while munching garlic cloves: What a feast!

Omelette provençale
Omelette provençal

For 4 servings:

- 8 eggs
- 3 sweet peppers
- 3 tomatoes
- 3 shallots
- 50 g (2 oz) black olives
- parsley
- salt, pepper
- 1 clove garlic
- 2 dessertspoons olive oil
- butter

Peel the shallots, prepare and slice peppers and gently stew in a frying pan with olive oil. Add the skinned tomatoes and chopped garlic. Reduce by cooking over a gentle heat for about 30 minutes and add the olives. Beat the eggs and cook the omelette with butter in a separate pan. Half-way through cooking, pour in half the stewed vegetables. Finish cooking the omelette and fold in half, using a palette knife. Add the remaining stewed vegetables to the pan.
Sprinkle with chopped parsley and serve immediately.

Oeufs brouillés
Scrambled eggs

For 6 servings:

- 10 new-laid eggs
- 2 dessertspoons double cream
- salt, pepper
- parsley
- croûtons

Break the eggs into a bowl and whisk briskly with a fork. Add a pinch of salt, a few turns of the peppermill, and the cream. Beat again and add some chopped sprigs of parsley. Pour the mixture into a saucepan and cook over a very gentle heat, stirring continuously with a wooden spoon. Watch carefully for the moment when the eggs begin to set, because they must keep their creamy consistency. It would be disastrous to cook for too long. Remove from the heat as soon as the mixture starts to thicken. Serve immediately with *croûtons*. This dish does not keep and must be served on hot plates as soon as it is ready. This excellent recipe makes an ideal entrée, a quick snack, or a good filling breakfast. The parsley may be replaced by chives and the pepper by grated nutmeg.

Anchoïade - *Provence*
Anchovy toasts

For 4 servings:

– **150 g (5 oz) anchovy fillets in oil**
– **100 g (3½ oz) butter**
– **100 g (3½ oz) purée of black olives**
– **1 clove garlic**
– **50 g (2 oz) dried breadcrumbs**
– **4 thick slices bread**
– **black olives**
– **tomatoes for decoration**

Pound the anchovies in a mortar, then add the butter and purée of black olives. This purée can be bought ready-made under the name 'Tapenade'. Alternatively it can be made by stoning 200 g (7 oz) olives and crushing them in a mortar. Mix all these ingredients together well to make a thick cream. Add the breadcrumbs and crushed garlic. Now toast the slices of bread on both sides. Spread the toast with the anchovy paste and put under the grill for a few seconds.
Decorate with a few black olives and tomato quarters.
Serve as an entrée or as a savoury snack with well-chilled rosé wine. This is an excellent recipe for an open-air meal, when the bread can be grilled over charcoal embers and spread with the purée while still hot.

Suggested wines:

Wine from Cassis, Côtes de Provence

Nouilles fraîches
Home-made noodles

For 6 servings:

– **350 g (12 oz) flour**
– **4 eggs**
– **2 pinches salt**

Sift the flour in a pile onto the table, make a hole in the centre, and add the eggs, salt, and a dessertspoon of cold water. Gently work the eggs into the flour with the fingers until a smooth dough is formed. Let the dough rest for an hour or two.
Roll out to a thickness of 3 mm (⅛ in) and cut into strips with a large knife. Leave the noodles on a kitchen towel to dry for a few hours and cook in salted boiling water.
Home-made noodles are a speciality of the Alsace region, where they are served with jugged hare and other dishes.

Pâté de Pâques - *Poitou-Vendée*
Easter pie

For 8 to 10 servings:

- 70 g (2½ oz) short pastry
- 3 very thick slices ham (approx. 300 g (11 oz))
- 800 g (1 lb 12 oz) sausage meat
- 6 eggs
- 300 g (11 oz) cooked spinach
- salt, pepper
- 50 g (2 oz) lard
- 200 g (7 oz) smoked bacon

Fold the lard into the short pastry and season with plenty of pepper. Hard-boil the eggs and cool under running water. Now, remove the outer leaves of the spinach and gently cook in a frying pan with small pieces of chopped bacon. Season the sausage meat with salt and pepper. Use about a third of the pastry to make a rectangular-shaped undercrust. Spread with a layer of sausage meat and place the slices of ham over. Cover with some of the spinach and top with the shelled eggs. Finally, layer with the remaining spinach and sausage meat.
Cover with pastry to form a shape like a large, elongated loaf. Seal the edges of the pastry firmly, decorate, and pierce a hole in the centre. Glaze with egg yolk and cook in the oven Mark 4, 350°F (180°C) for 2 hours, protecting the top of the pastry with a sheet of greased paper for the first hour of cooking.
Serve warm or cold.

Suggested wines:

Gros-Plant, Light Bordeaux

Fondue savoyarde
Fondue

For 6 servings:

- 1.3 kg (2¾ lb) Beaufort or Comté cheese
- 1 clove garlic
- salt, pepper
- 3 glasses dry white wine
- 1 liqueur glass kirsch

Grate the cheese fairly coarsely. Chop and crush the garlic in a fondue dish or metal skillet. Pour the wine in and heat. When the wine begins to boil, season with salt and pepper and gradually add the cheese. Stir with a wooden spoon over a low heat to melt the cheese into the wine. When cooked, the cheese should have absorbed all the wine, forming a smooth creamy mixture. Then add the kirsch and serve immediately.
The fondue dish should be kept hot at the table by means of a small spirit burner. Each guest soaks a piece of bread in the fondue with a long-handled fork. Hand a small glass of kirsch to each guest.
The fondue may be thickened with a teaspoon of cornflour blended with a little water, then added to the fondue, which prevents it from separating on cooling. A variety of cheeses are suitable for the fondue: Comté may be mixed with Beaufort: a little Vacherin may be added: or Swiss cheeses, like Gruyère or Emmentaler and Fribourg, may be used. In any case, always choose dry cheeses with a high fat content and a strong taste.

Suggested wines:

White wine from Savoy, Crépy

Canapés au roquefort
Roquefort cheese canapés

For 8 servings:

- 150 g (5 oz) Roquefort cheese
- 100 g (3½ oz) butter
- 3 dessertspoons brandy
- 25 g (1 oz) raisins
- 50 g (2 oz) green walnuts
- chives
- bread (farmhouse, wholemeal or toasting)

Mix the butter with the Roquefort cheese in a large basin, kneading together to form a smooth paste. Add the brandy, raisins, chopped green walnuts (but keep some whole for decoration) and chopped chives. Mix all the ingredients together. Cut the bread into slices. Spread these slices with the Roquefort mixture and decorate with green walnuts.
Serve as an appetiser or entrée.
The mixture of butter, Roquefort and brandy may be prepared beforehand. It then improves the taste that can be highlighted by seasoning with a little cayenne pepper. The walnuts and raisins are added at the last moment.

Croûte au fromage
Cheese crusts

For 6 servings:

- crusty loaf
- 200 g (7 oz) Gruyère cheese
- 2 eggs
- 50 g (2 oz) butter
- 25 g (¾ fl oz) double cream
- nutmeg
- chives
- salt and pepper

Cut six slices of bread, not too thick, and spread with butter. Then, grate the cheese and blend in a bowl with the cream and eggs. Season with salt and pepper and grate in a little nutmeg. Mix well together. Generously cover each slice of bread with this mixture and place under the grill until well browned.
Serve hot or warm sprinkled with chopped chives.

Suggested wine:

Dry white wine

Soufflé au fromage
Cheese soufflé

For 4–6 servings:

– 150 g (5 oz) Gruyère cheese
– $\frac{1}{2}$ l (1 pt) milk
–100 g (4 oz) plain flour
– 25 g (1 oz) butter
– salt and pepper
– 5 eggs

Coarsely grate the cheese. Make a very thick bechamel sauce with the milk, flour and butter. Season with salt and pepper. Add the cheese and stir well, heat gently until cheese has melted. Remove from the heat. Separate the egg whites from the yolks. Beat the yolks into the sauce. Whisk the egg whites until stiff, fold into the cheese mixture. Pour into a buttered 2$\frac{1}{2}$-3 pt soufflé dish. Cook in a moderate oven Mark 4, 350°F (180°C) for 45 minutes. Serve immediately.

Foie gras en brioche
Goose livers baked in brioche dough

▶

For 8 to 10 servings:

– 2 x 400 g (14 oz) fat goose or duck
  livers (foie gras)
– 2 truffles
– 2 l (3$\frac{1}{2}$ pt) chicken stock
– slices larding bacon
– salt, pepper
– 400 g (14 oz) brioche dough
– aspic jelly

Trim the fat livers, remove the sinews, and soak in salted water for 12 hours. Then season with salt and pepper. Tie the livers in muslin and simmer for 30 minutes in the chicken stock. Leave to cool in the stock. Meanwhile, prepare the brioche dough and use to line the base of a well-buttered rectangular cake tin. Remove the livers from the stock, drain, stud with the truffles and wrap in slices of larding bacon. Place these livers in the tin and cover with dough. Bake in the oven. When the brioche is cooked, take out and allow to cool.
Melt the aspic jelly and add 2 dessertspoons of juice from the truffles. With a syringe, fill the space left between the liver and the brioche with this jelly.
Serve cold and decorate with the remaining jelly.

Suggested wines:

Sauternes, Champagne

Tourte à la viande
Meat pie

For 6 servings:

- 500 g (1 lb 2 oz) short pastry
- 300 g (11 oz) cold boiled beef
- 300 g (11 oz) sausage meat with herbs
- 4 onions
- 50 g (2 oz) butter
- salt, pepper
- 1 egg yolk
- 1 bay-leaf

Line a fairly deep flan ring with the pastry. Peel and roughly chop the onions. Melt the butter in a frying pan and fry the onions on a medium flame. Meanwhile, roughly chop the meat. When the onions begin to colour, add the beef and sausage meat. Gently brown and season with salt and pepper. Add the chopped bay-leaf. Fill the lined flan ring with the meat and cover with pastry. Make a vent in the top and glaze with egg. Cook in the oven Mark 4, 350°F (180°C) for an hour and serve very hot.
Any type of meat may be used for this dish: veal, pork or even mutton. If using mutton, it is not necessary to add any sausage meat.
One of the meats should contain a small proportion of fat so that the pie will not be too dry.

Suggested wines:

Red Bordeaux or Burgundy

Pan bagnat - *Provence*
Savoury bread

For each serving:

- 1 round bread roll or a large hunk of French bread
- 3 dessertspoons olive oil
- 2 anchovies in oil
- 1 tomato
- 1 stick celery
- 1 dessertspoon flaked tuna
- 1 teaspoon lemon juice

Cut the bread in half and dampen both sides with olive oil. Chop and mix the ingredients and pile on one half of the bread. Sprinkle with lemon juice and add salt. Cover with the other piece of bread like a sandwich.

Suggested wines:

Rosé from Provence, Tavel

Cuisses de grenouilles - *Dombes*
Frogs legs

For 6 servings:

- 6 dozen frogs legs
- 2 eggs
- 6 cloves garlic
- 100 g (3½ oz) dried breadcrumbs
- salt, pepper
- 50 g (2 oz) parsley
- 150 g (5 oz) butter

Beat the eggs in a large basin. Chop the garlic and parsley and mix with the breadcrumbs. Season with salt and pepper. Dip the frogs legs in the beaten egg and then coat in breadcrumbs. Fry in butter and serve very hot.

Suggested wines:

Chablis, Sancerre

Escargots - *Bourgogne*
Snails

For 4 servings:

- 4 dozen snails
- court bouillon made with onion, carrot, garlic, thyme, bay-leaves, salt, pepper, 1 glass white wine
- 150 g (5 oz) butter
- 30 g (1 oz) parsley
- 6 cloves garlic
- salt, pepper

Choose Burgundy snails which have starved for a long time and are closed up by a hard seal. Wash and completely immerse in boiling water for 10 minutes. Remove the snails from their shells and cook in the prepared stock for 3½ hours. Allow to cool in the cooking liquor.
Prepare the sauce by working the butter with garlic, chopped parsley, salt and pepper. Put a snail into each shell and fill with this flavoured butter. Place the snails into an indented dish and cook in the oven Mark 4, 350°F (180°C) for 10 minutes.
Serve immediately.

Gâteau de crêpes aux champignons
Pancake gâteau with mushrooms

For 6 servings:

- 18 pancakes
- 300 g (11 oz) button mushrooms
- 50 g (2 oz) plain flour
- $\frac{1}{4}$ l ($\frac{1}{2}$ pt) milk
- 50 g (2 oz) butter
- salt, pepper
- 100 g ($3\frac{1}{2}$ oz) grated Gruyère cheese

Prepare 18 fairly thick pancakes in the traditional way and lightly season with salt. Keep hot. Prepare the mushrooms to remove the grit, or drain if canned. Brown the mushrooms in a frying pan with 25 g (1 oz) of butter. Now, make $\frac{1}{4}$ l ($\frac{1}{2}$ pt) of bechamel sauce with the flour, milk and remaining butter. Season with salt and pepper. When cooked first add the cheese, then the mushrooms. Place a pancake in an ovenproof dish, pour over a little of the bechamel sauce with mushrooms, then top with another pancake, and so on.
Reheat in the oven before serving.
This dish tastes even better if the bechamel sauce is made with equal parts of milk and cream.

Suggested wines:

Saint-Emilion or light Burgundy

Quiche lorraine
Egg and bacon tart

For 6 servings:

- 500 g (1 lb 2 oz) short pastry
- 100 g ($3\frac{1}{2}$ oz) smoked bacon
- 100 g ($3\frac{1}{2}$ oz) ham
- 25 g (1 oz) butter
- 4 eggs
- $\frac{1}{2}$ glass milk (just over 2 fl oz)
- $\frac{1}{2}$ glass double cream
- 2 dessertspoons plain flour
- salt, pepper
- nutmeg

Fold an egg into the pastry to line a fairly deep 20 cm (8 in) flan ring. Chop the smoked bacon and ham into small pieces and brown with butter in a frying pan. Beat together the eggs, milk, cream and flour. Add salt, pepper and a little grated nutmeg. Drain the bacon and ham and place on the pastry. Pour the eggs over and bake in a hot oven Mark 6, 400°F (200°C) for 30 minutes.
This dish may be varied by adding some pieces of Gruyère or Beaufort cheese with the bacon and ham. It all depends on individual taste.
Serve hot with green salad.

Suggested wine:

Pinot rouge from Alsace

Tarte au chou
Cabbage flan

For 6 servings:

– **500 g (1 lb 2 oz) short pastry**
– **300 g (11 oz) smoked bacon**
– **1 cabbage**
– **3 shallots**
– **salt, pepper**
– **50 g (2 oz) butter**

Remove the outer leaves of a good cabbage and blanch in salted boiling water for 30 minutes. Meanwhile, make a short pastry to line a 20 cm (8 in) flan ring. Finely chop the smoked bacon and shallots and cook in a very large frying pan with the butter. Fry gently until golden, but do not allow to colour too deeply. When the cabbage is blanched, drain and cut roughly with a knife. Place the cabbage in the frying pan, cover and cook, stirring from time to time. Season to taste and fill the pastry with this mixture.
Bake the flan in the oven Mark 4, 350°F (180°C) and serve hot, dotted with knobs of butter.

Suggested wine:

Red Burgundy

Tarte à l'oignon - *Alsace*
Onion flan

For 6 servings

– **500 g (1 lb 2 oz) short pastry**
– **500 g (1 lb 2 oz) medium sized onions**
– **100 g (3½ oz) smoked bacon**
– **25 g (1 oz) butter**
– **100 g (3 fl oz) double cream**
– **3 dessertspoons plain flour**
– **salt, pepper**

Line a 20 cm (8 in) flan ring with the pastry.
Now peel and roughly chop all the onions. Bake the pastry 'blind' in the oven until it begins to turn golden-brown. Put the butter with the finely chopped bacon into a frying pan. Gently fry for a while, then add the chopped onions and cook over a very gentle heat for 15 to 20 minutes without browning the onions. When they are soft, add salt, pepper and flour, stirring briskly. Remove from the heat and add the cream. Fill the flan with this mixture and bake in a moderate oven Mark 4, 350°F (180°C) for 30 minutes.

Suggested wine:

Dry white Alsatian wine: Riesling

Melon au jambon cru
Melon with ham

For 4 servings:

- **2 medium-sized melons**
- **16 slices good quality raw ham**

Cut the melons into slices and scoop out the pips. Serve each guest with the equivalent of half a melon and 4 thin slices of raw ham in a little side dish. The two are eaten together, but do not put the ham straight into the melon halves, as it tends to soak up the melon juice and loses its own taste. The choice of melons is very important. Personally, I choose them by smell, as with camembert. There is no need to arouse the greengrocer's anger by pressing the melon with the thumb. A good melon has a delicate fragrance when it is ripe; too strong a smell is the sign of an over-ripe melon.

Céleri rémoulade
Celeriac with mustard

For 6 servings:

- **1 celeriac**
- **salt, pepper**
- **3 dessertspoons vinegar**
- **2 dessertspoons mustard**
- **1 glass oil**

Peel and grate the celeriac. Add salt and moisten with 3 dessertspoons of vinegar. Allow to macerate in this dressing for an hour. Put 2 dessertspoons of mustard into a basin with a pinch of salt and a teaspoon of vinegar. Gradually add the oil, as with a mayonnaise. Just before serving, blend the grated celery with the dressing.
This dish makes an excellent first course in the winter. It may be served with beetroot and herb salad, leek salad or grated cabbage salad.

Saucisson en croûte - *Lyonnais*
Sausage in a pastry crust

For 4 servings:

– 1 large (approx 500 g (1 lb)) smoked cooking
  sausage
– 1 large packet frozen puff pastry (13 oz)
  (or make your own half puff paste)
– 1 egg yolk

Take a good smoked sausage and poach for 30 minutes in salted boiling water, and leave to cool. Roll out the half puff paste, that is to say, puff paste which has only been folded a few times. Take the sausage out of the water and remove its skin. Place on the pastry and roll up. Seal the edges, glaze with the egg yolk, and cook in a moderate oven Mark 7, 425°F (218°C) for 30 minutes.
Serve hot with salad as an entrée.

Suggested wines:

Bourgueil, Beaujolais

Rillettes
Potted pork

For 8 to 10 servings:

– 500 g (1 lb 2 oz) fresh lean pork
– 500 g (1 lb 2 oz) fat belly pork
– 100 g (3½ oz) goose or pork fat
– 500 g (1 lb 2 oz) goose meat
– 1 shallot
– 3 bay-leaves
– 1 sprig thyme
– salt, pepper

Melt the goose fat in a pot. Cut the meats into small pieces, and add with the shallot, thyme and bay-leaves. Season with salt and pepper. Cook for 4 hours over a very low heat, taking care not to boil. The meats should not be allowed to brown. Remove the bay-leaves and thyme. Drain the meats and pack into earthenware pots. Press down well and cover with the strained fat from the pot. Place greaseproof paper over the pots. Potted pork keeps very well if stored in a cool place.

Suggested wines:

Red Bordeaux or Burgundy

Oeuf à la coque
Soft-boiled egg

A soft-boiled egg is considered so simple to prepare that to write a recipe for it would seem to be pointless.

I do not agree, as it is not so easy as might appear to boil an egg well. I do not propose to detail the exact altitude at which an egg should be boiled, but there are a few simple rules to be followed which are not always apparent at first sight.

Primarily, the egg must be very fresh, preferably from a farm. Next, when gauging the cooking time, never use an egg straight from the refrigerator as, being cold, it will take longer to cook, or will burst. If using a refrigerated egg, give it time to reach room temperature. Boil the egg in water and not, as is sometimes done, in a soup or boiling broth. Gently put the egg into the water with a wooden spoon and place it on the bottom of the saucepan so that it does not break. If it is a large egg cook it for 3 minutes (for those who like part of the white to be milky) or $3\frac{1}{2}$ minutes (for those who like their whites well set).

Take the egg out of the water at the end of this time, slip it between two hot napkins, and serve immediately.

For the record, it should be noted that in the Middle Ages, eggs were eaten and opened on their sides.

Raclette - Savoie
Melted cheese with vegetables

For 8 servings:

- $\frac{1}{2}$ wheel semi-soft Raclette cheese (Bagnes or Conches)
- 1 kg (2 lb) potatoes
- 1 kg (2 lb) carrots
- 500 g (1 lb 2 oz) onions
- 500 g (1 lb 2 oz) turnips
- 100 g (4 oz) smoked bacon
- salt, pepper
- thyme, bay-leaves

Cook the peeled vegetables in water with the bacon, salt, pepper, thyme and bay-leaves.

Choose half a wheel of a strong, but not overfresh, Raclette cheese. Make a log fire in the hearth for the charcoal embers. Wash a thick wooden plank, about the size of the cheese. Just before serving, bring the vegetables in their stock to the table. Put the cheese on the plank and place near the embers.

Serve a few vegetables on each plate in turn and, using a large knife, scrape off the side of the cheese facing the fire as it melts.

This melted cheese dish may also be served with gherkins. The plates should be kept hot.

Do not invite more than 8 guests, otherwise they will have to wait too long between each scrape of the cheese.

Suggested wines:

Crépy, White wine from Savoy

2
Soups

Soupe au pistou - *Provence*
Vegetable soup flavoured with basil

For 6 servings:

– **300 g (11 oz) French beans**
– **150 g (5 oz) fresh white haricot beans**
– **150 g (5 oz) fresh red haricot beans**
– **3 potatoes**
– **4 tomatoes**
– **4 cloves garlic**
– **1 onion**
– **1 bunch fresh basil**
– **4 dessertspoons olive oil**
– **salt, pepper**

Peel the vegetables and skin the tomatoes. Cook in $2\frac{1}{2}$ l ($4\frac{1}{2}$ pt) of water, seasoned with salt and pepper. Meanwhile, in a mortar pound the chopped garlic and basil and add olive oil. Cook the soup for 45 minutes. Place the basil and garlic mixture in a soup-tureen and add the soup just before serving. This soup is traditionally served in large earthenware soup plates.

Aigo boulido - *Provence*
Boiled garlic soup

For 6 servings:

– **6 gloves garlic**
– **3 dessertspoons olive oil**
– **salt, pepper**
– **sage**
– **crusty farmhouse loaf**

Boil the crushed garlic with some sprigs of sage in 2 l ($3\frac{1}{2}$ pt) of water. Add salt and pepper. After 15 minutes, pour this liquid over slices of bread, which have been sprinkled with olive oil and placed in a soup-tureen.
Serve immediately.

Soupe de poissons
Fish soup

For 6 servings:

– 1 kg (2 lb) assorted fish:
  eels, rainbow wrasse, scorpion fish,
  (or any white fish)
– crabs
– 2 onions
– 2 tomatoes
– 3 cloves garlic
– 1 leek
– 1-2 bay-leaves
– some fennel (fresh or dry)
– 3 tablespoons oil
– salt, pepper
– croûtons

Place the oil in a pot and brown the sliced vegetables with the crushed garlic. Then add fennel, bay-leaves, fish and crabs. Allow to brown for 5 minutes, and pour in enough water to cover. Season with salt and pepper, and cook for 30 minutes on a high flame. Take out the crabs and extract the meat. Remove the bones from the fish and pass both vegetables and flesh through a shredder. Adjust the seasoning to taste and leave to boil for 5 minutes. Serve with *croûtons* rubbed with garlic and sprinkled with grated cheese.
Some recipes for fish soup recommend the addition of saffron. I prefer to leave it out and so keep this dish tasting of fish.

Soupe aux pâtes
Noodle soup

For 6 servings:

– 100 g (3½ oz) French beans
– 100 g (3½oz) green peas
– 2 medium sized onions
– 3 tomatoes
– 200 g (7 oz) carrots
– 1 tablespoon chopped parsley
– 100 g (3½ oz) noodles
– 25 g (1 oz) butter
– salt, pepper

Place the butter in a large saucepan and brown the chopped onions and carrots. Add the French beans, green peas, skinned and chopped tomatoes, and chopped parsley. Pour in 2 l (3½ pt) of water or stock, and cook for 30 minutes.
Then add salt, pepper and noodles. Cook until the noodles are ready (about 10 minutes) and serve.

Soupe de sud-ouest
Meat and cabbage soup

For 6 servings:

- 1 kg (2 lb 2 oz) salt pork
- 500 g (1 lb 2 oz) fresh green beans
- 500 g (1 lb 2 oz) broad beans
- 3 turnips
- 4 carrots
- 3 leeks
- 2 medium sized onions
- $\frac{1}{2}$ cabbage (500 g (1 lb 4 oz))
- 3 cloves garlic
- 4 cloves
- 1 pimento

Rinse the salt pork in running water and place in a pot with 4 l (7 pt) of water. Bring to the boil. Add the cabbage, green and broad beans and cook for 30 minutes. Then add the finely chopped turnips, carrots, leeks, onions and pimento, followed by garlic and cloves. Bring back to the boil, reduce the heat and simmer for $1\frac{1}{2}$ hours. Taste before seasoning as the salt pork may suffice to salt the soup.

Suggested wines:

Madiran, Cahors, Red Bordeaux

Soupe au fromage
Cheese soup

For 6 servings:

- 1 l (1$\frac{3}{4}$ pt) milk
- 1 l (1$\frac{3}{4}$ pt) stock (2 chicken stock cubes)
- 25 g (1 oz) butter
- 1 level tablespoon plain flour
- 150 g (5 oz) mature grated cheese
- 1 clove garlic
- salt, pepper
- 1 egg yolk
- chopped parsley

In a large saucepan heat the butter, then add the flour and cook over a low heat, stirring all the time until golden brown; add the stock and milk and bring to the boil, stirring. Turn down heat and simmer for 5 minutes; add cheese. In a small bowl mix egg yolk with a little of the hot soup, then add to the pan of soup; stir over a low heat for a few minutes, but it is important not to allow to boil. Season with salt, pepper and chopped garlic.
Serve sprinkled with parsley.

Bouillabaisse - *Provence*
Mediterranean fisherman's soup

For 6 servings:

- **3 kg (6 lb 6 oz) assorted fish:**
  scorpion-fish, eel, red mullet, turbot
  whiting, crawfish
- **2 leeks**
- **4 tomatoes**
- **3 medium sized onions**
- **3 cloves garlic**
- **parsley**
- **1 bay-leaf**
- **some fennel (fresh or dry)**
- **salt, pepper**
- **pinch saffron**
- **4 tablespoons olive oil**

Chop the vegetables: onions, leeks, tomatoes and garlic. In a large saucepan, slightly brown with the olive oil. When they begin to soften, add the pieces of fish. Cover with water and add finely chopped herbs, bay-leaf, salt, pepper and saffron.
Cook for 20 minutes. Serve the broth in a soup-tureen over slices of bread, with the fish on a separate dish.
This recipe incorporates several species of fish, including rockfish, crawfish, eels and others, but excluding oily fish.
Naturally, all these fish must be very fresh. Unfortunately, it is difficult to obtain them everywhere. (However, a good English version of this soup can be prepared with white fish, such as fresh cod or haddock).
Only by the Mediterranean can the true taste of a *bouillabaisse* be savoured.

Soupe à la lotte
Turbot soup

►

For 4 servings:

- **300 g (11 oz) turbot**
- **2 shallots**
- **2 tomatoes**
- **pinch saffron**
- **25 g (1 oz) butter**
- **1 glass white wine**
- **salt, pepper**
- **sprig of thyme**
- **bread**
- **garlic**

Clean the turbot, remove the skin, and cut into fairly small pieces. Place 2 l (3½ pt) of water in a saucepan with salt, pepper, thyme and saffron. Add the wine and chopped shallots.
Skin and pulp the tomatoes, and place in the soup with the turbot. Cook for 30 to 45 minutes. Add the butter just before serving. *Croûtons* rubbed with garlic go well with this delicately flavoured soup.

Potage au potiron
Pumpkin soup

For 6 servings:

– **500 g (1 lb 2 oz) pumpkin**
– **$\frac{3}{4}$ l (1$\frac{1}{4}$ pt) milk**
– **100 g (3 fl oz) double cream**
– **$\frac{1}{4}$ l ($\frac{1}{2}$ pt) stock**
– **salt, pepper**

Cook the pumpkin in boiling water seasoned with salt and pepper. Remove from the water and press through a sieve. Add the stock and milk to the pumpkin purée. Reheat, seasoning to taste, and add cream just prior to serving.

Soupe aux légumes et à l'orge
Vegetable soup with barley

For 6 servings:

– **4 leeks**
– **4 carrots**
– **3 shallots**
– **200 g (7 oz) lean beef**
– **100 g (3$\frac{1}{2}$ oz) barley**
– **salt, pepper**
– **bay-leaves**
– **2 l (3$\frac{1}{2}$ pt) water**

Peel the vegetables and chop into small pieces. Cut the meat into small cubes. Toss both meat and vegetable pieces into 2 l (3$\frac{1}{2}$ pt) of boiling water. Add salt, pepper and bay-leaves. Cover the pan and cook for 1 hour. Then add the barley, cook for a further 30 minutes, and serve.
Some bones, including a marrow bone, may also be added to this soup. They must, of course, be removed before serving.
The marrow from the bone tastes good on hot toast with salt and pepper.

Soupe aux moules
Mussel soup

For 4 servings:

– 2 l (3½ pt) mussels
– ½ l (1 pt) white wine
– 1 carrot
– 2 shallots
– parsley
– salt, pepper
– 50 g (1½ fl oz) double cream
– 25 g (1 oz) butter

Scrub the mussels and scrape off their beards, discarding any that do not shut tightly. Place in a large saucepan, cover and cook for about 10 minutes until the shells open. Remove from the heat as soon as they are open. Now peel and finely chop the carrots, shallots, and a large sprig of parsley. In another saucepan, fry the carrots and shallots in butter. Cook slowly so as not to brown. When the shallots are tender, add the white wine and continue cooking. Strain the mussels and add their liquor to the soup. Shell the mussels and add to the soup with the parsley. Pour in ½ l (1 pt) of water and bring to the boil. Season to taste.
Just before serving, take the saucepan off the heat and add the cream.

Soupe à l'oignon
Onion soup

For 6 servings:

– 6 large sized onions
– 50 g (2 oz) butter
– 1 l (1¾ pt) stock
– salt, pepper
– 6 slices bread
– 100 g (3½ oz) grated Emmentaler or Gruyère cheese

Peel and slice the onions. Melt the butter in a saucepan and gently cook the onions until golden brown. When they are soft, add the stock and simmer for 15 minutes. Season with salt and pepper. Arrange the slices of bread in an ovenproof soup-tureen and ladle the soup over. Sprinkle with grated cheese and bake in the oven until bread and cheese are golden brown.
This soup may be served in individual fondue dishes, floating a slice of bread in each.

Soupe à l'oeuf
Egg soup

For 4 servings:

– 1 l (1¾ pt) chicken stock
– 1 red pepper
– 2 cloves garlic
– 25 g (1 oz) butter
– 4 eggs
– 1 dessertspoon vinegar
– parsley

Slice the pepper and gently fry with butter in a shallow pan. After 10 minutes, add the chopped garlic and leave to brown for a further 5 minutes. Pour the contents of the pan into the stock and bring to the boil. Meanwhile, poach the eggs in water with vinegar added and put one into a dish for each guest. Sprinkle with parsley and cover with the stock and slices of pepper.

Potage aux poireaux
Leek soup

For 6 servings:

– 4 leeks
– 1 onion
– 3 potatoes
– salt, pepper
– butter
– 2 l (3½ pt) water

Wash the leeks, discarding the green leaves, and cut into small pieces. Peel the potatoes and onions. Place all the vegetables in 2 l (3½ pt) of water, and add salt and pepper. Cook for 45 minutes.
Pass through a vegetable-mill and serve with a large knob of butter.
This recipe can also be made without shredding the vegetables, in which case the potatoes must be finely diced and the onions sliced.

Potage à la tomate
Tomato soup

For 6 servings:

– 6 tomatoes
– 3 onions
– 2 cloves garlic
– chives
– thyme, bay-leaves
– pepper, salt
– 25 g (1 oz) butter
– 2 l (3½ pt) water

Skin the tomatoes. Melt the butter in a saucepan and add the chopped onions. When the onions are soft, but not too brown, add the tomatoes, garlic, chopped chives, thyme, bay-leaves, salt, and pepper. Pour in 2 l (3½ pt) of water and cook for 30 minutes.
Strain the soup through a sieve and serve.

Soupe aux pois cassés
Split pea soup

For 6 servings:

– 200 g (7 oz) split peas
– 4 carrots
– 3 medium sized onions
– 150 g (5 oz) smoked bacon
– 1 bay-leaf
– butter
– 50 g (1½ fl oz) double cream

Leave the split peas to soak overnight. Dice the bacon into small cubes and fry in a little butter. Peel and slice the onions and brown with the bacon. Drain the split peas and add to the bacon, along with the carrots cut into rounds, bay-leaf, salt, pepper, and 2 l (3½ pt) of water. Cook for 1½ hours. Press through a sieve and serve with cream.

Soupe aux champignons
Mushroom soup

For 6 servings:

– chicken bones
– 1 stick celery
– 200 g (7 oz) carrots
– 2 onions
– 2 turnips
– thyme, bay-leaf
– salt, pepper
– 50 g (2 oz) butter
– 200 g (7 oz) button mushrooms

Place the butter in a shallow pan and brown all the sliced vegetables, except for the mushrooms.
When everything has slightly coloured, add 1½ l (2½ pt) of water, the chicken bones, salt, pepper, thyme and bay-leaf. Cook over a medium flame for 45 minutes. Then add the sliced mushrooms and cook for a further 10 minutes.

Potée auvergnate

Auvergne peasant soup

For 6 servings:

- 1 kg (2 lb 2 oz) cabbage
- 500 g (1 lb 2 oz) smoked streaky bacon
- 250 g (9 oz) carrots
- 3 medium sized onions
- 3 turnips
- 6 small potatoes
- salt, pepper
- 3 l (5¼ pt) water

Wash the cabbage and blanch for 10 minutes in boiling water. Put the bacon, together with 3 l (5¼ pt) of water into a large pot. Cook for 1 hour. Skim. Then add all the vegetables except for the potatoes. Season with salt and pepper. Cook for a further 2 hours. Now add the peeled potatoes and continue cooking until they are done.

Soupe au chou-fleur

Cauliflower soup

For 6 servings:

- 1 cauliflower
- 50g (1½ fl oz) double cream
- 1 dessertspoon cumin
- 2 egg yolks
- salt, pepper
- parsley
- croûtons

Blanch the cauliflower in a pot of boiling water for 30 minutes. Remove from the water and drain. Plunge into 2 l (3½ pt) of boiling water, seasoned with salt, pepper and the dessertspoonful of cumin. Cook for a further 30 minutes. Pass this soup through a vegetable mill. Blend the cream with the egg yolks and add to the soup just before serving.
Serve with *croûtons* and parsley.

Soupe aux haricots et aux choux
Bean and cabbage soup

For 6 servings:

– 1 kg (2 lb 2 oz) green cabbage
– 200 g (7 oz) dried beans
– 2 onions
– 2 carrots
– 2 bay-leaves
– salt, pepper
– 100 g (3½ oz) smoked bacon
– cheese

Soak the beans overnight in unsalted water. Blanch the cabbage in boiling water for 15 minutes and drain. Put cabbage, beans, peeled carrots, salt, pepper and bay-leaves into a pot with 3 l (5¼ pt) of water. Cook for 1½ hours. Just before serving, cut the bacon into small pieces and brown in a frying pan.

Roughly chop the cabbage and serve the soup. Let each guest help himself to a little grated cheese and pieces of diced bacon.

This soup makes an excellent main course meal in winter.

Soupe au lait
Milk soup

For 6 servings:

– 1 l (1¾ pt) milk
– 1 l (1¾ pt) chicken stock
– 2 cloves garlic
– 6 slices bread

Boil the stock with crushed garlic for 10 minutes. Add the milk and heat, without bringing to the boil. Toast the slices of bread and place in the soup-tureen.

Pour the soup over and serve.

Potage au cresson
Watercress soup

For 6 servings:

– 1 large bunch watercress
– 3 small potatoes
– salt, pepper
– 125 g (3¾ fl oz) double cream

Sort and wash the watercress. Peel the potatoes. In a saucepan containing 2 l (3½ pt) of water, put salt, pepper, diced potatoes, and two-thirds of the watercress. Cook until the potatoes are soft. Then add the remainder of the watercress and remove from the heat. Pass the soup through a vegetable mill. Add a spoonful of cream to each plate just before serving.

3
Vegetables

Chou rouge aux pommes
Red cabbage with apples

For 6 servings:

- 1.5 kg (3 lb 4 oz) red cabbage
- 6 cooking apples
- 1 medium sized onion
- 1 glass red wine
- 2 dessertspoons lard
- salt, pepper
- bay-leaves

Melt the lard in a pot, add the chopped onion, and gently fry until brown. Meanwhile, wash and roughly chop the red cabbage. Put into the pot and cook in the red wine. Add two apples, peeled and diced, and bay-leaves. Season well with salt and pepper. Cook over a low heat for 1½ hours. Check that the cabbage does not stick to the bottom of the pot. If necessary, add a little more wine.
When cooked, add the 4 remaining apples, peeled and quartered. Continue cooking for a further 15 minutes, and serve with fried sausages, grilled pork chops or roast pork.

Cèpes à la provençale
Flap mushrooms provençal

For 6 servings:

- 1.5 kg (3 lb 4 oz) flap mushrooms (Boletus edulis) (tinned)
- 2 tomatoes
- 1 shallot
- 2 cloves garlic
- chopped parsley
- thyme
- 50 g (2 oz) butter
- 3 tablespoons oil
- salt, pepper

Peel and wipe, but do not wash the mushrooms. Leave the caps intact and cut the stalks into pieces. Fry together with chopped shallot and crushed tomatoes in a mixture of butter and oil, and season with salt and pepper. Chop the herbs and garlic and add to the pan as soon as the mushrooms are cooked.
Serve immediately.

Suggested wines:
Saint-Emilion, Pomerol, Corbières

Purée de carottes
Carrot purée

For 6 servings:

- 1 kg (2 lb) carrots
- 2 small potatoes
- 1 glass milk
- salt, pepper
- 2 tablespoons parsley
- 25 g (1 oz) butter

Cook the peeled carrots in well-salted water. Half-way through cooking, add the potatoes. When the vegetables are cooked, drain carefully. Press through a sieve and add the milk and butter.
Sprinkle with chopped parsley just before serving.

Tarte aux tomates
Tomato flan

For 6 servings:

- **500 g (1 lb 2 oz) short pastry**
- **1 kg (2 lb) tomatoes**
- **3 eggs**
- **1 tablespoon plain flour**
- **50 g (1½ fl oz) double cream**
- **salt, pepper**
- **thyme**

Line a well-buttered 25 cm (10 in) flan ring with the pastry. Swiftly plunge the tomatoes into boiling water so that they can be peeled easily. Cut the tomatoes in half and place on the flan pastry. Beat together the eggs, flour and cream. Add salt, pepper and a sprig of thyme. Pour this mixture over the tomatoes. Cook in a moderate oven Mark 4, 350°F (180°C) for 30-45 minutes. Serve warm or cold.
This dish has a delicious flavour when made with fresh tomatoes, but canned tomatoes may also be used.

Poireaux au jambon
Leeks with ham

For 4 servings:

- **1.5 kg (3 lb 4 oz) leeks**
- **200 g (7 oz) sliced ham**
- **100 g (3½ oz) Gruyère cheese**
- **⅓ l (½ pt) bechamel sauce**
- **nutmeg**
- **salt, pepper**
- **25 g (1 oz) butter**

Wash the leeks and discard the green leaves. Cook whole in plenty of salted water. Add a little pepper and half a grated nutmeg to the bechamel sauce. Arrange the leeks in a buttered ovenproof dish. Roughly dice the ham and add to the sauce. Pour this sauce over the leeks, taking care to cover completely. Sprinkle grated cheese over this dish and dot with knobs of butter. Brown in the oven.
This dish may be enriched by adding fresh double cream to the bechamel sauce.

Lentilles aux saucisses
Lentils with sausages

For 6 servings:

– 500 g (1 lb 2 oz) lentils
– 3 smoked sausages
– 3 medium sized onions
– 200 g (7 oz) carrots
– salt, pepper
– 2 bay-leaves
– 100 g (3½ oz) bacon

Wash and cook the lentils with the peeled carrots, onions, and bacon. Season with salt and pepper, add 2 bay-leaves and cover with water. Cover the pan and cook on a low flame for 1½ hours. Plunge the smoked sausages into boiling water for 15 minutes and place on top of the lentils and other vegetables to serve.
This recipe may be prepared in the same way, using salt pork in place of the sausages. The salt pork is rinsed and cooked with the lentils, so there is no need to add salt.

Suggested wine:

Red Burgundy

Purée de pois cassés aux saucisses
Split pea purée with sausages

For 4 servings:

– 1 kg (2 lb 2 oz) split peas
– 4 frying sausages
– 1 smoked sausage
– 200 g (7 oz) carrots
– 1 medium sized onion
– 1 stick celery
– salt and pepper
– croûtons

Soak the split peas overnight.
Peel the onion and carrots. Put the split peas, onion, carrots, stick of celery, salt and pepper into a saucepan and cover with water. Cook for an hour, then add the smoked sausage. Just before serving, fry the sausages in a frying pan, put the carrots to one side, and make a purée with the split peas, onion and celery.
Serve with *croûtons*.

Suggested wines:

Côtes du Rhône, Corbières

Chou-fleur à la crème
Cauliflower with cream sauce

For 6 servings:

- 1.5 kg (3 lb 4 oz) cauliflower
- 3 eggs
- $\frac{1}{4}$ l ($\frac{1}{2}$ pt) double cream
- nutmeg
- salt, pepper
- croûtons

Wash a good cauliflower and remove the outer leaves. Cook whole in plenty of salted boiling water. Hard-boil and shell the eggs. Fry the bread cubes in oil. Thoroughly drain off the cooking liquor, and place the cauliflower in the serving dish. Garnish with quarters of egg and cover with the cream, heated (but not boiled) with salt, pepper and nutmeg.
Serve with the *croûtons*.
This recipe is delicious when made with a good, fresh cauliflower, as it retains all its flavour. It is most important to cook the cauliflower in plenty of water.

Ragoût d'aubergines
Aubergine stew

For 6 servings:

- 200 g (7 oz) bacon rind
- 1.5 kg (3 lb 4 oz) aubergines
- 8 cloves garlic
- salt, pepper
- 2 dessertspoons chopped parsley .
- 2 glasses red cooking wine

Cover the bottom of a casserole dish with the bacon rind. On top, place unpeeled halves of aubergine. Add the garlic, parsley, salt and pepper, and moisten with red wine. Cover and braise for an hour.
(Aubergines are more bitter unless their cut surface is sprinkled with salt; they should be left to drain for about $\frac{1}{2}$ hour, then rinsed under fresh water).

Choucroute - *Alsace*
Sauerkraut garnished with bacon and sausages

For 6 servings:

- 1.5 kg (3 lb 4 oz) fresh sauerkraut
- 150 g (5 oz) larding bacon
- 250 g (9 oz) streaky bacon
- 1 large smoked sausage
- 1 knuckle ham
- 6 Strasbourg sausages or Frankfurters
- 1 medium sized onion
- 1 carrot
- 1 bottle white wine
- peppercorns
- juniper berries
- 50 g (2 oz) goose fat
  (other fats may be used)

Buy fresh sauerkraut. Wash and squeeze dry. Line the base of a casserole dish with larding bacon. Cover first with a layer of sauerkraut then with the streaky bacon, knuckle of ham, smoked sausage, carrot, onion, peppercorns and juniper berries. Add another layer of sauerkraut, moisten with white wine, and spread over with goose fat.
Cover the pan and cook in the oven Mark 4, 350°F (180°C) for 3-4 hours. When cooked, add the Strasbourg sausages. Serve with boiled potatoes.
Sauerkraut lends itself to various meats. For example, the knuckle of ham may be replaced by goose, duck, or grilled pork chops, added separately at the last moment.

Suggested drink:

Riesling, Sylvaner or pale ale

Papeton de poivrons - *Provence*
Peppers provençal

For 6 servings:

- 1 kg (2 lb 2 oz) sweet peppers
- 6 eggs
- 100 g (3 fl oz) double cream
- salt, pepper
- 1 clove garlic
- 20 g ($\frac{3}{4}$ oz) butter

Wash and prepare the peppers, and cut into quarters lengthways. Poach for 15 minutes in salted boiling water. Meanwhile, liberally butter a mould. Blend the eggs with the cream and add chopped garlic. Season with salt and pepper. Line the mould with quarters of pepper and fill with any remaining pieces. Pour the egg mixture into the mould and cook in a bain marie at Mark 4, 350°F (180°C). After 1 hour insert a knife or needle. If clean it is cooked.
Turn out and serve hot.

Suggested wine:

Rosé from Provence

Chou rouge aux marrons et au lard
Red cabbage with chestnuts and bacon

For 6 servings:

- 1.5 kg (3 lb 4 oz) red cabbage
- 1 kg (2 lb 2 oz) chestnuts
- 1 slice larding bacon
- 250 g (9 oz) smoked bacon
- 1 dessertspoon vinegar
- 1 apple
- salt, pepper

Wash and roughly chop the cabbage. Poach the chestnuts to remove their skins. Line the base of a pot with a slice of larding bacon, and over this spread a mixture of cabbage, chestnuts and diced apple. Moisten with the vinegar and a glass of water. Season with salt and pepper. Cover and cook for 1½ hours. Thinly slice and grill the smoked bacon and add just prior to serving.
This vegetable dish is ideal with goose or turkey.

Haricots rouges au lard et saucisses
Red beans with bacon and sausages

For 6 servings:

- 1 kg (2 lb 2 oz) red haricot beans
- 2 smoked sausages (240 g (8½ oz) each)
- 300 g (11 oz) smoked bacon
- 3 medium sized onions
- 2 bay-leaves
- salt, pepper
- 1 carrot

Soak the red beans overnight. Peel the carrot and onions. Place the beans, carrot, onions, bacon, bay-leaves, salt and pepper in a saucepan. Cover with water and cook for 1½ hours. Then add the sausages and cook for a further 30 minutes.
Serve straight from the saucepan.

Suggested wine:

Red Burgundy

Endives au jambon

Chicory with ham

For 6 servings:

– 6 large heads chicory
– 6 slices ham
– 150 g (4½ fl oz) double cream
– salt, pepper

Poach the chicory heads in salted boiling water for 15 minutes. Drain thoroughly. Roll each head of chicory in a slice of ham.
Arrange in a buttered ovenproof dish. Add salt and pepper, and cover with the cream. Bake in a very hot oven Mark 8, 450°F (232°C) for 15 minutes.

Navets au gratin

Turnips baked with cream

For 4 servings:

– 600 g (1 lb 5 oz) turnips
– ¼ l (½ pt) bechamel sauce
– 100 g (3 fl oz) double cream
– nutmeg
– salt, pepper
– 50 g (2 oz) butter
– 50 g (2 oz) Gruyère cheese

Peel the turnips and cook for 30 minutes in boiling water. Meanwhile prepare a bechamel sauce, seasoning well with salt, pepper and grated nutmeg. Add the cream. Drain the turnips and place in a well-buttered, ovenproof dish. Cover with sauce and grated cheese. Arrange a few knobs of butter over the cheese and brown in the oven.
The turnip is a somewhat ill-favoured vegetable. This recipe restores the cheap and neglected turnip to its rightful place.

Navets au jus

Stewed turnips

For 6 servings:

– 600 g (1 lb 5 oz) small turnips
– 100 g (3½ oz) butter
– salt, pepper
– 1 cup meat stock

Choose small, young turnips. Peel. Heat the butter in a casserole dish and gently brown the turnips. Season with salt and pepper. After cooking for 35-40 minutes, add the meat stock and cook for a further 5 minutes.
Serve the turnips to accompany roast meat.

Gratin dauphinois

Potatoes baked with milk

For 6 servings:

– 2 kg (4 lb 4 oz) potatoes
– 50 g (2 oz) butter
– 1 glass milk
– salt, pepper
– 1 clove garlic

Peel and thinly slice the potatoes. Butter an ovenproof dish and layer with potato slices. Sprinkle each layer with salt, a little chopped garlic, and one or two turns of the pepper-mill. Pour the milk over. Bake in a hot oven Mark 6, 400°F (200°C) for 45-60 minutes or until soft.
There are numerous recipes for this dish, which is subject to more controversy than the renowned *cassoulet* (French bean pot stew)—see p. 111.
Some people add neither milk nor garlic. The Savoy version includes strong Beaufort cheese and more garlic than the other recipes. Another variation advocates the use of fresh cream. I have even found a recipe in which the milk is replaced by white wine! Whichever recipe is used, it is important that the potatoes are well cooked and soft for the dish to be at its best.

Pommes sarladaises
Sarlat potatoes

For 6 servings:

– 1 kg (2 lb 2 oz) potatoes
– 200 g (7 oz) truffles
  (less can be used)
– 4 dessertspoons goose fat
  (other fats may be used)
– salt and pepper

Peel and thinly slice the potatoes. Melt the goose fat in a frying pan. Cook the potatoes in this pan with salt and pepper. When half cooked, add the sliced truffles and continue cooking until brown.

Courgettes à la provençale
Courgettes with tomatoes

For 6 servings:

– 6 courgettes
– 6 tomatoes
– 3 cloves garlic
– parsley
– salt, pepper
– olive oil

Peel the courgettes, place in a casserole dish, and lightly toss in oil. When the courgettes are almost cooked, add the tomatoes cut into halves. Season with salt and pepper and leave to brown. Turn the tomatoes, taking care not to squash. When they are cooked, sprinkle with chopped garlic and parsley, and serve immediately.

Suggested wine:

Rosé wine from Provence

Épinards à la crème
Creamed spinach

For 4 servings:

– 1.5 kg (3 lb 4 oz) spinach
– 50 g (2 oz) butter
– nutmeg
– salt
– 150 g (4½ fl oz) double cream

Prepare and wash the spinach. Cook for 10 minutes in salted boiling water and drain thoroughly. Finely chop with a knife or pass through a vegetable shredder. Place the butter in a saucepan and add the spinach. Cook for 10 minutes to evaporate the excess water. Season with salt and grated nutmeg. Add the cream just before serving.
Creamed spinach may be served with *croûtons*.

Cèpes à la persillade

Flap mushrooms in parsley sauce

For 6 servings:

- **1 kg (2 lb 2 oz) mushrooms, preferably cèpes**
- **50 g (2 oz) butter**
- **2 dessertspoons oil**
- **1 cup chopped parsley and chives**
- **4 cloves garlic**
- **salt, pepper**

Wash and peel the mushrooms. Dry well and cut into pieces. Gently fry in the oil and butter for 30 minutes. Then add the chopped garlic and cook for a further 10 minutes. Now, season with salt, pepper and chopped herbs. Leave to brown for five minutes and serve.

Haricots paysanne

Country style beans

For 6 servings:

- **1 kg (2 lb 2 oz) fresh haricot beans**
- **200 g (7 oz) carrots**
- **3 medium sized onions**
- **4 tomatoes**
- **2 turnips**
- **4 potatoes**
- **150 g (5 oz) ham on the bone**
- **100 g (3½ oz) butter**
- **salt, pepper**
- **thyme, bay-leaf**
- **3 cloves garlic**

Put the butter to melt in a cast iron casserole dish. Add the chopped garlic, sliced onions, with turnips and carrots cut into rounds. Allow to colour, then add the peeled and pulped tomatoes, diced ham, potato cubes and haricot beans. Season with salt and pepper, and add the thyme and bay-leaf. Moisten with a glass of water. Cover and braise for 45 minutes.

Aubergines frites

Fried aubergines

For 6 servings:

- 4 aubergines
- 2 onions
- 2 cloves garlic
- salt, pepper
- 1 glass oil
- chives

Heat the oil and toss in the aubergines cut into rounds. (See footnote on page 57). When cooked on both sides, remove from the oil and keep warm. Then cut the onions into rounds and fry. Arrange the aubergines on a plate, and sprinkle with chopped garlic and chives. Season with salt and pepper and top with the fried onions.

Chou rouge aux saucisses

Red cabbage with sausages

For 6 servings:

- 1.5 kg (3 lb 4 oz) red cabbage
- 2 cooking apples
- 2 shallots
- $\frac{1}{2}$ bottle red wine
- salt, pepper
- 2 dessertspoons goose fat
- 2 smoked sausages (or 6 Frankfurters)

Melt the goose fat in a casserole dish and add the chopped shallots. Meanwhile, wash and roughly shred the red cabbage. Brown the cabbage with the shallots. After 15 minutes, add quarters of apple, salt, pepper and red wine. Cover and cook over a low flame for 40 minutes.
Poach the sausages and arrange on the cabbage just before serving.

Rizotto

Risotto

For 6 servings:

- 600 g (1 lb 5 oz) rice
- 2 sweet peppers
- 2 medium sized onions
- 200 g (7 oz) smoked bacon
- 100 g (3½ oz) olives
- ½ glass oil
- salt, pepper
- thyme
- fresh fennel
- ½ l (1 pt) stock

Heat the oil in a cast-iron casserole dish. Prepare the peppers and slice into thin strips. Skin and chop the onions. Fry both onions and peppers in the oil. Then add the smoked bacon cut into small pieces. When everything is well browned, pour in the rice and allow to colour slightly. Add salt, pepper, chopped fresh fennel and thyme. Moisten with stock and cook gently until the rice has soaked up all the liquid.
When cooked, add the olives.

Tomates farcies aux champignons

Tomatoes with mushroom stuffing

For 6 servings:

- 6 large tomatoes
- 150 g (5 oz) button mushrooms
- 100 g (3½ oz) cooked ham
- ¼ l (½ pt) thick bechamel sauce
  (1 oz butter, 1½ oz flour, ½ pt milk)
- 1 egg yolk
- 50 g (2 oz) cheese
- salt, pepper
- butter
- parsley

Cut the tops off the tomatoes and with a teaspoon scoop out the seeds. Place the tomatoes in a buttered ovenproof dish. Now, make a thick bechamel sauce and add the grated cheese, washed and diced mushrooms and chopped ham. Season with salt and pepper and add the egg yolk. Fill the tomatoes with this stuffing and cook for 10 minutes in a hot oven, Mark 6, 400°F (200°C).
Sprinkle with parsley just before serving. This can be used as a starter.

Tomates farcies charcutière
Tomatoes with pork stuffing

For 6 servings:

- 6 tomatoes
- 200 g (7 oz) minced pork
- 2 eggs
- 100 g (3½ oz) dried breadcrumbs
- 50 g (2oz) butter
- 1 dessertspoon chopped parsley
- salt, pepper

Cut the tops off the tomatoes and scoop out the seeds. Put a pinch of salt in each tomato. Mix the minced pork, breadcrumbs, eggs and chopped parsley. Add salt and pepper and fill the tomatoes with this stuffing. Put a small knob of butter on each tomato and place in an ovenproof dish. Cook in the oven, Mark 4, 350°F (180°C) for 30 minutes.

Suggested wine:

Beaujolais

Aubergines farcies
Stuffed aubergines

For 6 servings:

- 3 aubergines
- 3 spring onions
- 1 tablespoon parsley
- chives and marjoram
- 3 eggs
- 3 dessertspoons double cream
- salt, pepper

Wash the aubergines and simmer for 15 minutes in boiling water. (See footnote on page 57). Drain and cut into two lengthways. Scoop out some of the flesh from each aubergine half and chop up. Chop the herbs and onions. Mix the chopped vegetables with the eggs, cream, salt and pepper. Also add salt and pepper to the inside of the aubergine shells and fill with the stuffing. Bake in the oven Mark 4, 350°F (180°C) for 30 minutes. If there is any stuffing left, it may be arranged around the aubergines in the dish.
Serve hot.

Pommes de terre frites
Chipped potatoes

For 6 servings:

– 2 kg (4 lb 4 oz) potatoes
– salt
– cooking oil

Peel the potatoes. Cut lengthways into small sticks. Wash and dry in a kitchen cloth. Heat the oil in a deep fryer. Put the potatoes into very hot oil and remove with a skimmer when they are crisp and golden.
It is bad practice to keep on using the oil remaining in the fryer. The ideal would be to change the oil each time, but this would be too costly. Therefore, in order to use the same oil several times over, leave to cool and strain through a fine muslin cloth.

Purée de pommes de terre
Creamed potatoes

For 6 servings:

– 2 kg (4 lb 4 oz) potatoes
– $\frac{1}{2}$ l (1 pt) milk
– 50 g (2 oz) butter
– salt

Peel and quarter the potatoes. Place in a saucepan of salted, cold water and cook. Drain, press through a sieve, and beat with a wooden spoon. Put the pan back on the heat and gradually add the cold milk, stirring all the time. Just before serving add the butter. Season with salt to taste.
Creamed potatoes should be quite stiff, particularly when served with meat and gravy. It is important to choose the right sort of potatoes: they should not disintegrate in boiling water, nor should they absorb too much water. Creamed potatoes should never be thinned with their own cooking liquor.

Couronne de pommes de terre
Potato ring

▶

For 6 servings:

– 2 kg (4 lb 4 oz) potatoes
– 250 g (9 oz) onions
– 50 g (2 oz) butter
– 1 clove garlic
– salt, pepper
– $\frac{1}{2}$ teaspoon paprika
– 150 g (4$\frac{1}{2}$ fl oz) double cream
– flour

Peel and coarsely grate the potatoes. Skin and chop the onions and garlic. Mix the vegetables together and thoroughly work in the flour. Add salt and pepper. Butter a ring mould and fill with the mixture. Arrange knobs of butter all around. Bake in a hot oven Mark 6, 400°F (200°C) for an hour. Serve with the cream seasoned with paprika.

Pommes de terre lyonnaises
Sauté potatoes with onions

For 6 servings:

– 1.5 kg (3 lb 4 oz) potatoes
– 3 onions
– salt, pepper
– 6 dessertspoons oil
– parsley

Peel and cut the potatoes into rounds. Skin and slice the onions. Heat the oil in a frying pan, toss in the potatoes and fry, turning occasionally; then add the onions. When the potatoes are golden-brown, season with salt and pepper, and sprinkle with parsley just before serving.

Haricots à la tomate
French beans with tomatoes

For 5 servings:

– 1 kg (2 lb 2 oz) fresh French beans
– 4 tomatoes
– 3 dessertspoons goose fat
  (other fats may be used)
– salt, pepper
– 50 g (2 oz) Gruyère cheese
– 1 medium sized onion
– 1 clove garlic

Cook the French beans in salted water. When they are almost cooked, but still firm, drain. Mix the beans with the raw tomatoes, sieved to a purée, and the chopped onion. Add the chopped garlic and season with salt and pepper to taste. Mix well, then add the goose fat. Fill an ovenproof dish with this mixture.
Sprinkle with grated Gruyère cheese and bake for 30 minutes in a very hot oven Mark 8, 450°F (232°C).

Mojettes à la crème - *Charente-Poitou*
White beans in cream sauce

For 4 servings:
– 1 kg (2 lb 2 oz) white beans or large fresh haricot
  beans
– 1 dessertspoon oil
– 25 g (1 oz) butter
– salt
– 150 g (4½ fl oz) fresh double cream
– stock

Melt the butter in a casserole or an earthenware dish. Add the oil and fry the beans for a few minutes. Moisten with the stock, cover, and cook for 3 hours. After cooking for 2 hours add salt. Drain, spoon the cream over the beans and serve.

Couronne de légumes en gelée
Vegetable ring in aspic jelly

For 6 servings:

- carrots
- French beans
- green peas
- stick celery
- turnips
- rice
- ham
- 400 g (1 lb) prepared aspic jelly
- gherkins
- salt, pepper

Cook the vegetables in salted water, observing their appropriate cooking times, so that they do not disintegrate. Cook the rice. Chop the ham and vegetables into small cubes, mix together and season with salt and pepper. Fill a ring mould with all the ingredients and pour the melted aspic jelly over. Leave to cool and set, then turn out just before serving.
Serve with gherkins, green salad and mayonnaise.
For best results, use only fresh spring vegetables and good quality aspic jelly in this dish. On no account use canned vegetables.
It is important not to overcook the vegetables so as not to impair their delicate taste.

Fonds d'artichauts aux pointes d'asperges
Artichoke hearts with asparagus tips

For 8 servings:

- 8 artichoke hearts (tinned)
- 3 eggs and 1 yolk
- 250 g (9 oz) asparagus tips
- salt, pepper
- oil
- parsley
- 1 dessertspoon cream

Cook the artichokes and trim to extract the hearts. If fresh artichokes are not available, canned artichoke hearts may be used, but the recipe will lose some of its flavour.
Leave the hearts to cool and meanwhile hard-boil the 3 eggs. Remove the shells and finely chop. Cook the asparagus tips and drain, keeping the best to one side. Cut the others up small and add to the chopped eggs, together with a little chopped parsley. Make a mayonnaise with oil and egg yolk; add salt and a dessertspoon of fresh cream. Mix half this mayonnaise with the chopped egg and garnish each artichoke heart with this dressing.
Pour the remaining mayonnaise over and decorate with the reserved asparagus tips. Both the artichokes and asparagus can be cooked the night before. The dish can then be quickly prepared before the meal.

Soufflé aux champignons
Mushroom soufflé

For 6 servings:

- **200 g (7 oz) mushrooms**
- **5 dessertspoons plain flour**
- **$\frac{1}{2}$ l (1 pt) milk**
- **50 g (2 oz) butter**
- **5 eggs**
- **50 g (2 oz) cheese**
- **salt, pepper**

Wash and peel the mushrooms. Chop up small with a knife. Prepare a thick bechamel sauce with the butter, milk and flour. Add salt, pepper and grated cheese. Break the eggs and separate the whites from the yolks. Fold the yolks into the sauce. Whisk the whites to a snow. Add the chopped mushrooms to the bechamel sauce and then gently fold in the egg whites.
Pour into a buttered soufflé dish and cook in a hot oven Mark 6, 400°F (200°C) for about 15 minutes.
Thyme may be added to the bechamel sauce in place of the cheese.

Tourte aux champignons
Mushroom tart

For 6 servings:

- **short pastry**
- **500 g (1 lb 2 oz) mushrooms**
- **250 g (9 oz) smoked bacon**
- **200 g (7 oz) ham**
- **1 dessertspoon plain flour**
- **2 eggs**
- **1 egg yolk for glazing**
- **3 dessertspoons double cream**
- **salt, pepper**

Prepare the short pastry to line a well-buttered oven-proof dish. Reserve some of the pastry for the pie lid. Now, prepare the mushrooms. Chop the bacon into small pieces and brown in a frying pan. Cook the mushrooms in the resulting bacon fat. Season with salt and pepper. When the mushrooms are well browned, remove from the heat, add the flour, and briskly stir. Then, while still off the heat, add the chopped ham and the 2 eggs blended with cream. Pour this preparation into the dish lined with pastry and cover with the remaining pastry. Make a vent in the lid and glaze with egg yolk.
Cook in the oven Mark 4, 350°F (180°C) for 1 hour. Serve hot.
This pie may be prepared in advance: it tastes just as good reheated. It goes very well with a green salad.

Suggested wines:

Red Burgundy or Bordeaux

Chou farci
Stuffed cabbage

For 6 servings:

- 1 large cabbage
- 250 g (9 oz) minced pork
- 200 g (7 oz) ham
- 1 medium sized onion
- slice larding bacon
- thyme, bay-leaves
- salt, pepper
- 50 g (2 oz) butter
- 1 glass white wine
- garlic

Wash the cabbage in plenty of water. Cook for 10 minutes in salted boiling water. Rinse and drain. Open the cabbage leaf by leaf, and remove the heart. Brown the pork and chopped ham in a frying pan with butter and chopped onion. Season with salt and pepper. When everything is well-browned, add the chopped cabbage heart. Cook for a little longer. Add thyme, bay-leaves, and a touch of chopped garlic. Fill the cabbage with this stuffing and tie up with string so that the leaves completely enclose the stuffing. Put the slice of bacon into a pot or a terrine. Place the cabbage on top. Moisten with white wine, cover, and cook in a moderate oven, Mark 4, 350°F (180°C) for an hour.

Suggested wines:

Bourgogne, Beaujolais, Côtes du Rhône

Tourte au chou
Cabbage tart

For 6 servings:

- 500 g (1 lb 2 oz) short or puff pastry
- 1 kg (2 lb 2 oz) cabbage
- 200 g (7 oz) smoked bacon
- 25 g (1 oz) butter
- nutmeg
- salt and pepper
- 1 egg yolk

Prepare the short or puff pastry and leave to rest. Remove the outer leaves from the cabbage and blanch in boiling salted water for 15 minutes. Remove from the water, drain, and chop with a knife. Cut the bacon into small pieces and fry with butter in a large frying pan. When the bacon is well browned, put the cabbage to cook with the bacon. Stir occasionally and allow the cabbage to slightly colour.
Line a 25 cm (10 in) mould with three-quarters of the pastry. Season with salt and pepper; grate a little nutmeg over the cabbage, and fill the pastry case. Cover with the remainder of the pastry, glaze with the egg yolk, and bake for an hour in a moderate oven.

4
Fish and shellfish

Daurade au fenouil - *Provence*

Sea bream with fennel

For 4 servings:

– 1 kg (2 lb 2 oz) sea bream
– fresh fennel stalks
– salt
– oil

Gut, wash and prepare the sea bream. Drain well and dry.
Start the fire well in advance if you wish to grill the fish over charcoal. Stuff the insides of the fish with the fennel stalks. Oil the sea bream on both sides and sprinkle with salt. Arrange the fish on a grill surrounded with fennel. Cook slowly over a gentle heat. Baste with oil, if necessary, during cooking. When cooking the fish under an oven grill, do not put fennel around the fish.

Suggested wine:

Dry white wine

Daurade au four

Baked sea bream

For 4 servings:

– 1.2 kg (2 lb 8 oz) sea bream
– 25 g (1 oz) butter
– 2 dessertspoons oil
– 3 shallots
– 1 branch fennel (dried or fresh)
– thyme, bay-leaves
– salt, pepper
– 4 tomatoes
– 1 glass dry white wine

Gut, scale and wash the sea bream. Stuff with the fennel, bay-leaves and thyme. Place the fish in an ovenproof dish and arrange tomato halves around. Chop the shallots and scatter over the fish and tomatoes. Season with salt and pepper, and sprinkle with oil and wine.
Bake in a moderate oven Mark 4, 350°F (180°C) for 40 minutes and baste from time to time during cooking. Serve straight from the baking dish.

Suggested wines:

Muscadet, Sancerre

Chaudrée

Fish broth with wine

For 6 servings:

- 1.5 kg (3 lb 4 oz) fish: plaice, eels, cod, red mullet
- 50 g (2 oz) butter
- 1 medium sized onion
- 4 cloves garlic
- salt, pepper
- $\frac{1}{2}$ l (1 pt) white wine
- good bunch parsley
- croûtons

Melt the butter in a saucepan. Add the chopped garlic, onion and parsley. Gently brown. Wash, gut and cut the fish into pieces. Place in the saucepan and season with salt and pepper. Add the white wine and top up with sufficient water to just cover the fish. Bring to the boil over a high heat and cook until the fish is done. Serve with *croûtons*.

Suggested wines:

Gros Plant, Muscadet

Soufflé au poisson

Fish soufflé

For 4-6 servings:

- 250 g (10 oz) fish
  (coley, or cod, salmon etc. could be used)
- $\frac{1}{2}$ l (1 pt) milk
- 100 g (4 oz) plain flour
- 50 g (2 oz) butter
- 4 eggs
- salt and pepper
- pinch of nutmeg

Steam or poach the fish, reserve any stock or juice. Remove skin and any bones from fish and flake with a fork. Make the juices from the fish up to $\frac{1}{2}$ l (1 pt) with the milk. Make a very thick bechamel sauce using the milk mixture, flour and butter. Separate the eggs and add yolks, salt and pepper, nutmeg, and fish to sauce, mix well. Whisk egg whites until stiff, fold into the fish mixture. Pour into buttered 2½-3 pt soufflé dish. Cook in a moderate oven Mark 4, 350°F (180°C) for about 45 minutes. Serve immediately.

Coquilles Saint-Jacques provençales
Scallops provençal

For 6 servings:

– 24 scallops in shells
– 4 cloves garlic
– 50 g (2 oz) butter
– 1 dessertspoon oil
– salt, pepper
– 2-3 tablespoons plain flour
– lemon
– 50 g (2 oz) dried breadcrumbs
– 1 tablespoon chopped parsley

Wash the scallop shells, retaining only the scallop and coral. Drain well and dip in flour. Melt the butter and oil in a frying pan and cook the scallops until golden. Season with salt, pepper and crushed garlic when well browned. Replace the scallops in their shells, sprinkle with breadcrumbs and chopped parsley, and place under the grill until brown. Serve with lemon.

Suggested wines:

Dry white or light Bordeaux

Coquilles Saint-Jacques à l'ail
Scallops with garlic

For 4 servings:

– 12 scallops
– 50 g (2 oz) butter
– 8 cloves garlic
– 1 glass white wine
– salt, pepper
– parsley
– 100 g (3 fl oz) double cream

Open the scallop shells, wash, and retain only the scallop and coral. Gently brown the scallops in a frying pan, taking care not to deepen the colour of the butter. Add the chopped garlic, two good handfuls of chopped parsley, wine, salt and pepper. Allow to simmer gently for 20 minutes. Add the cream just before serving.

Suggested wines:

Dry white wine or light Bordeaux

Filets de sole normande

Fillets of sole normande

For 4 servings:

– 2 soles, cut into fillets
– ½ l (1 pt) mussels
– 100 g (3½ oz) shrimps
– 100 g (3½ oz) mushrooms
– ½ l (1 pt) dry white wine
– 1 shallot
– 50 g (2 oz) butter
– 100 g (3 fl oz) double cream
– 2 egg yolks
– salt

Wash the fillets of sole. Now scrape and rinse the mussels and shake open over a sharp heat. Retain the liquor from the mussels. Place the butter and chopped shallot in a large saucepan. Brown slightly over a gentle heat. Add the wine, the liquor from the mussels chopped mushrooms, and peeled shrimps. Cook for 15 minutes over a low heat. Remove the shrimps and mushrooms and poach the fillets of sole in this stock. Remove the sole and arrange in a dish with the shelled mussels, the mushrooms and shrimps. Reduce the cooking liquor, salt if necessary, and thicken with the egg yolks and cream. Cover the fish with this sauce.

Suggested wines:

Meursault, Chablis or Pouilly fuissé

Couronne de sole

Ring of sole

For 6 servings:

– 12 fillets sole
– 50 g (2 oz) butter
– 1 tablespoon plain flour
– 1 shallot
– bouquet garni
– 200 g (8 oz) peeled shrimps
– 50 g (1½ fl oz) double cream
– salt, pepper
– saffron

Wash the fillets of sole. Put the fish bones and heads into a saucepan with a little water, salt, pepper, the shallot and *bouquet garni*. boil and reduce to obtain a very strongly flavoured stock. Strain this stock and leave to cool. Now, generously butter a ring mould and fill with the fillets of sole. Cook over a saucepan of water (*bain marie*) for 40 minutes. Meanwhile, make a white *roux* with the butter, flour and fish stock. Add the cream and a dash of saffron, and adjust the seasoning. Then add the peeled shrimps.
Turn out the mould onto a hot plate and pour the sauce over.
Garnish with shrimps.
(Fillets of whiting may also be used for this recipe).

Suggested wines:

Pouilly Fumé, Chablis

Sardines frites

Fried sardines

For 4 servings:

- **20 fresh sardines**
- **3 or 4 tablespoons plain flour**
- **salt**
- **frying oil**
- **lemon**
- **parsley**

Scale, gut and wash the sardines, which should be very fresh. Then dry and roll in flour. Fry in very hot oil and serve with salt and lemon juice, garnish with parsley. In France, fresh sardines may be bought at port auctions. They lie on the decks of the trawlers, still silvery and glistening with salt water.

Rougets au fenouil

Red mullet with fennel

For 6 servings:

- **6 red mullets**
- **$\frac{1}{2}$ head fennel**
- **50 g (2 oz) butter**
- **2 or 3 branches fennel**
- **2 shallots**
- **$\frac{1}{2}$ glass dry white wine**
- **salt**

Gut, scale and wash the red mullet. Heat the butter in a shallow pan and add the chopped fennel and shallots. Cook gently without allowing to brown. Then add the salt and white wine. Put the fennel into an ovenproof dish.
Place the fish on top and pour the shallots and fennel in their cooking liquor over. Place in a moderate oven at Mark 4, 350°F (180°C) for 30 minutes, and serve.

Suggested wine:

Dry white wine

Rougets à la tomate
Red mullet with tomatoes

For 5 servings:

- 5 red mullets
- oil
- 3 tomatoes
- 3 cloves garlic
- $\frac{1}{2}$ glass dry white wine
- 1 lemon
- salt and pepper
- parsley

Gut, scale and wash the red mullet. Brush with oil and grill or cook in a frying pan. In the meantime, cook the tomatoes to make a tomato sauce, and add crushed garlic, salt, pepper and white wine. Strain this sauce through a fine sieve, and serve with the red mullet.
Garnish with lemon and parsley.
It is important to use well-ripened tomatoes and a non-acid wine for the sauce, or it will be too sharp.

Suggested wine:

Dry white wine

Turbot sauce hollandaise
Turbot with hollandaise sauce

For 4 servings:

- 1 kg (2 lb 2 oz) piece of turbot
- bouquet garni
- salt, pepper
- 3 egg yolks
- 150 g (6 oz) butter
- 1 lemon
- court-bouillon

Gut the turbot, remove the black skin, and wash. Cook in the prepared fish stock with the *bouquet garni*. While this is cooking, place the three egg yolks with 3 dessertspoons of water in a small saucepan. Heat this over a pan of water and gradually work in the butter, stirring with a wooden spoon. When all the butter has melted and the sauce has thickened, remove from the heat, add salt, pepper and lemon juice, and serve in a sauce-boat to accompany the turbot.
This dish goes well with boiled potatoes.

Suggested wines:

Pouilly Fumé, Meursault, Sancerre

Brandade de morue

Creamed salt cod

For 6 servings:

- 500 g (1 lb 2 oz) salt cod
- 2 cloves garlic
- olive oil
- milk
- bouquet garni
- hard boiled eggs
- 6 slices bread

Overnight soak the salt cod in several changes of water. Simmer the cod for about 15 minutes with the *bouquet garni*, but do not allow to boil. Take out of the water when cooked and remove the skin and bones.
Flake the cod in a saucepan and crush this fish with a wooden spoon over a very gentle heat, gradually adding a little olive oil and milk until an oily white cream is obtained. Adjust the seasoning, add the chopped garlic, and serve on fried bread squares, with slices of hard boiled egg.

Morue aux haricots rouges

Cod with red beans

For 6 servings:

- 500 g (1 lb 2 oz) fresh red beans
- 500 g (1 lb 2 oz) de-salted cod
- 50 g (2 oz) dried breadcrumbs
- 1 egg
- salt, pepper
- red and green peppers
- cooking oil

Cook the red beans in salted water for 45 minutes. Meanwhile, drain the cod, which has been well soaked to remove the salt. Cut into small squares, dip in the beaten egg and then in the breadcrumbs. Season with pepper and deep fry. Serve these pieces of fried cod on a bed of drained red beans, with chopped peppers.
If using dried beans, leave to soak overnight and cook for a little longer.

Suggested wine:

Rosé from Provence

Morue en aïoli - *Provence*
Salt cod in garlic mayonnaise

For 6 servings:

- 1.5 kg (3 lb 4 oz) salt cod
- 3 courgettes
- 6 carrots
- 3 heads fennel
- 500 g (1 lb 2 oz) French beans
- 1 cauliflower
- 6 potatoes
- 3 tomatoes
- 1 beetroot
- 8 eggs
- 1 medium sized onion
- salt, pepper
- olive oil
- 4 cloves garlic
- thyme, bay-leaves

Soak the salt cod overnight, changing the water at least three times; 24 hours later, cook the cod in plenty of water with the thyme, bay-leaves and onion. Similarly cook the carrots, courgettes, fennel, cauliflower, French beans and potatoes in plenty of salted water. Cook the beetroot separately. Hard-boil 6 of the eggs. Then prepare a mayonnaise with the 2 remaining eggs and flavour with the 4 crushed garlic cloves reduced to a pulp. Season with salt and pepper.
Serve the flaked salt cod in a dish. The beetroot is diced and served with the raw tomatoes, cut in half, and the hard-boiled eggs. The cooked vegetables are placed in another dish and the garlic mayonnaise is handed separately. The vegetables used in this dish may be varied according to the season, but they must be very fresh.

Suggested wines:

White or rosé wines from Provence

Morue provençale
Salt cod provençal

For 4 servings:

- 500 g (1 lb 2 oz) salt cod
- 6 tomatoes
- 2 cloves garlic
- 2 shallots
- 3 dessertspoons oil
- salt, pepper
- thyme, bay-leaves
- 1 tablespoon chopped parsley
- black olives

The day before, soak the cod in several changes of water. Heat the oil in a shallow pan and add the quartered tomatoes, chopped garlic, shallots and parsley with the thyme, bay-leaves, salt and pepper. Leave to simmer for a few minutes, then add the pieces of cod. Cover and cook over a gentle heat for 30 minutes. Add the black olives just before serving.

Suggested wine:

Rosé wine from Provence

Bouilleture d'anguille

Eels in white wine

For 6 servings:

- 1.5 kg (3 lb 4 oz) eels
- 2 medium sized onions
- 100 g (3½ oz) butter
- ½ bottle dry white wine
- salt, pepper
- 200 g (6 fl oz) double cream
- 1 handful of spinach

Cut the eels into portions. Place the butter in a shallow pan and brown the eels and chopped onions. When the pieces of eel have browned, add the chopped spinach with the white wine and cook over a gentle heat for 20 minutes. Season with salt and pepper and remove the pieces of eel. Reduce the cooking liquor to half quantity and thicken with the cream before returning the eels to the pan.
Keep hot until ready to serve, taking care not to boil.

Suggested wines:

Gros-Plant, Muscadet, Riesling

Maquereaux aux vin blanc

Mackerel in white wine

For 5 servings:

- 5 small mackerel
- 2 bay-leaves
- 1 onion
- 1 shallot
- 1 carrot
- 1 l (1¾ pt) white wine
- salt
- peppercorns

Fillet the small mackerel and arrange in an earthenware terrine. Prepare a marinade with the white wine, onion, carrot and finely chopped shallot. Add salt, bay-leaves and peppercorns. Bring to the boil and pour immediately over the mackerel. (It is important that the wine is boiling as this 'cooks' the fish). Cover and leave to marinate in a cool place for 48 hours before serving.

Suggested wines:

Muscadet, Gros-Plant

Maquereaux à la crème

Mackerel in cream sauce

For 4 servings:

- 8 small mackerel
- 2 shallots
- 50 g (2 oz) butter
- ½ glass dry white wine
- salt, pepper
- plain flour
- 100 g (3 fl oz) double cream
- parsley

Gut and wash the mackerel. Coat with flour. Peel and chop the shallots. Now, put the shallots to soften into a casserole dish with butter. Cook gently for 10 minutes, taking care not to brown. Then moisten with white wine, season with salt and pepper, and add the mackerel. Cook over a medium heat, turning the fish to cook well on both sides. When the fish are cooked, remove from the casserole dish and keep hot in the serving dish. Thicken the cooking liquor with the cream, add a little chopped parsley, and pour this sauce over the fish just before serving.

Suggested wines:

Muscadet, Sancerre

Maquereaux à la moutarde

Mackerel with mustard

For 5 servings:

- **5 small mackerel**
- **1 pot strong Dijon mustard**
- **1 dessertspoon plain flour**
- **salt, pepper**
- **1 lemon**
- **oil**

Wash and clean the mackerel and dry well. Mix the mustard with the flour and add seasoning. Coat each fish with this blend of flour and mustard and place between the bars of a double grill. Pour a little oil over each fish and cook on charcoal or under a grill, on both sides. Serve with wedges of lemon.

Suggested wine:

Dry white wine

Harengs saurs à la crème

Smoked herrings in cream

For 6 servings:

- **12 fillets of smoked herring**
- **2 medium sized onions**
- **1 glass oil**
- **4 peppercorns**
- **50 g (1½ fl oz) cream**

Place the smoked herring fillets to marinate in the oil for 48 hours, together with an onion cut into rings and the peppercorns. At the end of this time, drain the herrings and onion and place in a serving dish with the other, finely chopped onion and the cream.
Serve with toasted bread.

Harengs marinés

Marinated herrings

- **smoked herrings**
- **onions**
- **thyme, bay-leaves**
- **peppercorns**
- **carrots**
- **oil**

Place the fillets of smoked herring in an earthenware bowl with onion rings, fresh thyme and bay-leaves, peppercorns, and carrots cut into rounds. Pour in oil to cover all the ingredients. Leave to marinate for several days.
These marinated herrings are good eaten with buttered toast.
They may also be served with boiled potatoes.
On the Normandy coast, they are eaten for breakfast.
These herrings keep well for several days.

Brochet à la crème
Pike in cream sauce

For 6 servings:

– 1 pike or salmon trout 2 kg (4 lb)
– 6 shallots
– 50 g (2 oz) butter
– ½ bottle dry white wine
– salt, pepper
– 1 carrot
– parsley
– 1 medium sized onion
– bay-leaves
– 1 egg yolk
– 200 g (6 fl oz) double cream

Gut, wash and remove the head from the pike. Place the fish head in ½ l (1 pt) of water to boil with the carrot, onion, parsley and bay-leaves. Reduce the resulting fish stock (*court bouillon*) to a half. Place the fish in a buttered, ovenproof dish. Add the chopped shallots, season with salt and pepper, and moisten with the white wine and reduced stock. Cover and cook in the oven. When the fish is cooked, keep hot and reduce the liquor to half. Strain the liquor and thicken with the cream and egg yolk, check the seasoning and pour this sauce over the fish.

Suggested wines:

Chablis, Pouilly Fumé

Moules au citron
Mussels with lemon

For 4 servings:

– 3 l (5 pt) mussels
– 100 g (3½ oz) carrots
– 3 shallots
– 50 g (2 oz) butter
– 1 dessertspoon plain flour
– salt, pepper
– bouquet garni
– 4 lemons
– ½ glass dry white wine
– parsley

In a shallow pan gently brown the grated carrots and chopped shallots with butter. While these are cooking, open the mussels in a saucepan over a fierce heat. Retain the liquor from the pan. When the shallots and carrots are nicely browned, sprinkle with flour, stir well, and moisten with the juice from the lemons, the pan liquor, and the white wine. Season with salt and pepper, add the *bouquet garni*, and leave to cook for 10 minutes over a gentle heat.
Just before serving, pour this sauce over the mussels and garnish with parsley.

Suggested wines:

Muscadet, Gros-Plant

Moules frites

Fried mussels

For 4 servings:

- 2 l (3½ pt) mussels
- 100 g (3½ oz) butter
- 100 g (3½ oz) soft bread
- 2 dessertspoons oil
- 6 cloves garlic
- salt, pepper
- 3 tablespoons parsley

Wash and scrape the mussels. Cook in a pan of water over a sharp heat to open. When fully open, drain, and retain only those halves of the shells containing the mussels. Heat the butter and oil in a large frying pan. Place the mussels in the pan and brown gently. Add the crumbled bread and blend with the chopped garlic. Season with salt and pepper, and gently brown, turning constantly, until the bread is crisp. Then add the chopped parsley and serve very hot.

Suggested wine:

Muscadet

Moules à la crème

Mussels with cream sauce

For 4 servings:

- 2 l (3½ pt) mussels
- 2 shallots
- 1 glass dry white wine
- 100 g (3 fl oz) double cream
- pepper
- 1 dessertspoon parsley
- 25 g (1 oz) butter

Wash and scrape the mussels. Place them in a large saucepan, cover and cook over a sharp heat until they open. Remove from the heat and retain the liquor from the pan. Strain this liquor. Cook the chopped shallots in butter until they are transparent, then add the white wine, the pan liquor, and pepper. Reduce slightly. Remove from the heat, add the cream and some chopped parsley, and pour this sauce over the hot mussels.

Suggested wines:

Muscadet, Gros-Plant

Brochettes de moules

Skewered mussels

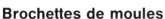

For 6 servings:

– 1½ l (2½ pt) large mussels
– 10 thin slices smoked bacon
– 2 very thick slices ham
– 2 eggs
– 100 g (3½ oz) dried breadcrumbs
– 100 g (3½ oz) butter
– salt, pepper
– 1 lemon

Open the mussels in a dry saucepan over a fierce heat. Remove from the shells. Wrap each mussel in a piece of smoked bacon. Cut the ham into cubes. Impale the ham and mussels on small skewers. Dip the skewers into the beaten eggs. Remove the skewers, season, and coat with breadcrumbs. Brown the skewers in butter in a frying pan over a moderate heat. Serve with lemon.

Suggested wine:

Dry white wine

Palourdes grillées

Grilled clams

For 6 servings:

– 6 dozen clams
– 4 shallots
– 100 g (3½ oz) soft bread
– 200 g (7 oz) grated Gruyère cheese
– 25 g (1 oz) butter
– 50 g (1½ fl oz) double cream
– 1 tablespoon parsley
– 2 glasses dry white wine

To open the clams, place a dry saucepan over an intense heat. Remove the clams and retain their juice. Put the butter and chopped shallots into a saucepan. Cook the shallots until transparent, taking care not to brown. Add the juice from the clams and the white wine. Allow this liquor to reduce to half, then add the crumbled bread and the cheese. Mix well. Remove from the heat. Chop the parsley and add to the mixture. Then finally stir in the cream.
Fill the clams with this stuffing and grill.

Huîtres à la bordelaise
Oysters bordelaise

For 4 servings:

- **4 dozen oysters**
- **12 truffled crepinettes or small frying sausages**
- **dry white wine or light red Bordeaux**

Open the oysters. Grill the sausages and serve with the oysters. A piece of sausage is eaten with each oyster. It is worth noting that many of those devoted to this style of eating oysters recommend accompanying the dish with a light red Bordeaux wine. However, it may also be served with a dry white wine.
(Crepinettes are little sausages made from minced meat and truffles, wrapped in strips of fat bacon, and baked or fried.)

Huîtres farcies
Stuffed oysters

For each serving:

- **1 dozen oysters**
- **50 g (2 oz) butter**
- **50 g (2 oz) dried breadcrumbs**
- **$\frac{1}{2}$ clove garlic**
- **1 cup chopped parsley**

Open the oysters and place in an ovenproof dish. Blend the chopped garlic and parsley into the softened butter. Add the breadcrumbs or crumbled bread. Put a teaspoonful of this mixture into each oyster and place under the grill. Serve immediately.

Suggested wines:

Muscadet, Gros-Plant or light red Bordeaux

Homard à l'armoricaine
Lobster breton

For 4 servings:

- 2 live lobsters
- 150 g (6 oz) oil
- 6 shallots
- 2 tomatoes
- ½ bottle dry white wine
- brandy
- salt, pepper
- bouquet garni

Drop live lobsters into boiling water for no more than 5 minutes; dry the lobsters, cut them into pieces and reserve the coral, creamy parts. Cook the pieces of lobster with butter in a shallow pan until golden-brown. Season with salt, pepper, and add the chopped shallots. Flame with brandy and add the wine. Add the skinned and seeded tomatoes and the mixed herbs. Cover and cook for 30 minutes over a gentle heat. Then remove the lobster pieces, pound the reserved coral and milky parts, and add with the liquid. Allow to reduce for 15 minutes.
Coat the lobster pieces in the sauce and serve with rice.

Homard à la normande
Lobster à la normande

For 4 servings:

- 2 lobsters
- 250 g (7½ fl oz) fresh double cream
- 25 g (1 oz) plain flour
- 3 shallots
- 50 g (2 oz) butter
- salt, pepper
- 1 sherry glass Calvados (Apple brandy)

Plunge the live lobsters into boiling water for no more than 5 minutes. Drain and split in half lengthways. Retain the creamy parts in a bowl. Lightly fry the lobsters in butter. When they are cooked, remove from the pan. Brown the chopped shallots in the pan. Off the heat, add the flour, then the cream. Season with salt and pepper and pour in the Calvados. Heat gently. Return the lobster pieces to the sauce for a few minutes, and add the creamy parts from the bowl.
Serve very hot.

Truite au bleu
Blue trout

For each serving:

– 250 g (9 oz) live trout
– bouquet garni
– 1 shallot
– 25 g (1 oz) butter

Gut and wash the trout as soon as it has been killed. Prepare a fish stock (*court bouillon*) with the shallots and mixed herbs. Plunge the trout into this fish stock for about 10 minutes, without allowing to boil. Remove the trout and serve immediately with melted butter.

Suggested wine:

Dry white wine

Truites aux amandes
Trout with almonds

For 4 servings:

– 4 trout, each weighing 250 g (9 oz)
– 100 g (3½ oz) flaked almonds
– 2 tablespoons plain flour
– milk
– 100 g (4 oz) butter
– 1 lemon
– salt, pepper

Gut and wash the trout. Dry well, dip in milk, then roll in flour. Season with salt and pepper. Melt 25 g (1 oz) of the butter in a frying pan and cook the trout until golden-brown. Heat the remaining butter in a separate pan to slightly brown the almonds.
Arrange the trout in a dish and pour the almonds and butter over just before serving.
Serve with boiled potatoes and lemon.

Suggested wines:

White Meursault, Pouilly-Fumé

5
Meats

Steak au poivre
Pepper steak

For each serving:

– 1 slice fillet steak
– 25 g (1 oz) butter
– salt
– peppercorns
– 50 g (1½ fl oz) double cream
– 1 teaspoon brandy

Crush the peppercorns, taking care not to grind into a powder. Sprinkle over each side of the meat and beat with a large spoon to press the pepper into the meat. Add salt and fry with butter in a frying pan. When cooked medium rare, remove the steak from the pan.
Flame the meat juices with brandy and thicken with cream.
Spoon this sauce over the steak and serve.

Suggested wine:

Full-bodied red Burgundy

Pot-au-feu
Beef broth

For 6 servings:

– 1.5 kg (3 lb 4 oz) meat
  (shin of beef, chuck, top rib,
  shoulder: any 2 of these cuts)
– 1 large smoked cooking sausage
– 1 marrow bone
– 200 g (7 oz) carrots
– 200 g (7 oz) turnips
– 3 leeks
– ½ cabbage
– 2 large onions
– 1 clove
– parsley, thyme, bay-leaves
– salt, pepper

Put 4 l (7 pt) of water into a large pot, season with salt and pepper, and add both the meat and marrow bone. Bring to the boil and cook for an hour, removing the scum as it rises. Add the sausage, and then the vegetables, peeled and left whole. Tie together the thyme, bay-leaves and parsley. Add this bunch of herbs (*bouquet garni*) and the clove to the beef broth. Cook for a further 2½ hours over a low heat.
Serve the broth in a soup-tureen, and the meat and vegetables separately, with several kinds of mustard.

Suggested wines:

Brouilly, Saint-Amour, Bourgueil

Côte de boeuf grillée
Grilled rib of beef

For 2 servings:

– 1 rib beef
– rosemary
– salt, pepper
– oil

Prepare a fire with charcoal or embers. Season the rib of beef with salt and pepper, sprinkle with chopped rosemary, and beat to press the rosemary into the meat. Brush the meat with oil. Place on the grill, not too near the fire. Grill on both sides. Serve with mustard.

Meat grilled over a charcoal fire is often cooked too quickly and is consequently liable to be burnt. This is because the meat is put directly into the flame or else placed too near the embers. For best results, the meat should be grilled gently, and be crisp without being burnt.

Suggested wines:

Pommard, Nuits-Saint-Georges, Red Beaune

Entrecôte marchand de vin
Rib steak with wine sauce

For 4 servings:

– 500 g (1 lb 2 oz) rib steak
– 3 glasses red wine
– 4 shallots
– 2 dessertspoons chopped parsley
– 1 lemon
– 2 dessertspoons reduced meat stock
– 150 g (5 oz) butter

Place the wine in a saucepan with the peeled and chopped shallots. Reduce until very little of the liquid remains. Fry the rib steak and add the stock off the heat. Work the butter until soft and add the shallots, chopped parsley and lemon juice. Generously spread this butter over the rib steak and serve.

Suggested wines:

Brouilly, Beaujolais, Châteauneuf-du-Pape

Steak tartare

Steak tartare

For each serving:

– 200 g (7 oz) fillet steak
– 1 egg yolk
– 1 tomato
– 2 dessertspoons chopped onion
– capers
– mustard
– parsley
– salt, pepper
– tomato sauce with pimentos

For this recipe, the meat is eaten raw, so it is advisable when buying a piece of fillet steak either to mince it at home or have the butcher mince it in your presence in order to be sure that it is fresh. Never use either frozen or ready prepared minced meat. Place the meat in the centre of each plate; the egg yolk in a half shell; and the vegetables and condiments around the meat. The meat is eaten after being blended with the egg, seasoned with salt and pepper, and spiced with condiments.
This dish goes well with chipped potatoes.

Suggested wines:

Bordeaux, Burgundy

Boeuf en gelée aux carottes

Beef in aspic jelly with carrots

For 6 servings:

– 1.5 kg (3 lb 4 oz) aitch-bone or
  fillet of beef
– 1 kg (2 lb 3 oz) carrots
– 150 g (5 oz) fat bacon
– 200 g (7 oz) button onions
– salt, pepper
– 250 g (9 oz) prepared aspic jelly
– butter

Lard the fillet of beef with strips of fat bacon. If you do not have a larding-needle, have your butcher prepare it for you. In a casserole dish, brown the meat on all sides with butter. Then add the carrots and onions, peeled and sliced. Season with salt and pepper. Moisten with 3 dessertspoons of water, cover and cook. After about 2 hours, when the meat is very tender, remove from the casserole dish, keeping the carrots and onions to one side, and skim the cooking liquor. Cut the cooked carrots into rounds and use to line a mould into which a little aspic jelly has been poured.
Place the meat over the carrots. Blend the skimmed meat stock with melted jelly and pour over the meat until the mould is full. The mould should be almost the same size as the piece of meat, so that not too much aspic jelly is used.
Leave to cool, then turn out. Reheat the remaining carrots and onions and serve with some gherkins.

Suggested wine:

Beaune

Boeuf en cocotte

Beef casserole

For 6 servings:

– **1.5 kg (3 lb 4 oz) fillet of beef**
– **3 carrots**
– **100 g (3½ oz) mushrooms**
– **150 g (5 oz) smoked bacon**
– **2 dessertspoons oil**
– **salt, pepper**
– **1 glass white wine**

Fry the meat in oil to brown on all sides. Peel and cut the carrots into rounds. Prepare and quarter the mushrooms. Finely dice the bacon. Add the carrots, mushrooms, bacon and wine to the meat. Season with salt and pepper. Cover and cook for 2 hours.
Serve with creamed potatoes or French beans.

Suggested wine:

Red Burgundy

Boeuf miroton

Beef hash with gherkins

For 4 servings:

– **600 g (1 lb 5 oz) top rib of beef boiled in broth**
– **½ glass Chablis wine**
– **2 dessertspoons vinegar**
– **1 dessertspoon concentrated tomato purée**
– **3 medium sized onions**
– **6 gherkins**
– **50 g (2 oz) butter**
– **50 g (2 oz) cheese**
– **salt, pepper**

Melt the butter in a casserole dish and add the sliced onions and chopped gherkins. Moisten with the white wine and vinegar and add the tomato concentrate. Season with salt and pepper and cook for 10 minutes. Cut the meat into thick slices and arrange in an ovenproof dish. Pour the sauce over, sprinkle with grated cheese, and brown in the oven. Serve very hot.
This dish uses up the left-overs from a beef broth (see *Pot-au-Feu* p. 98.)

Suggested wine:

Light Burgundy

Daube de boeuf

Beef stew with wine

For 8 servings:

– 1.5 kg (3 lb 4 oz) rump or aitch-bone of beef
– 200 g (7 oz) fat bacon
– 200 g (7 oz) bacon rind
– 5 medium sized onions
– 6 carrots
– 2 cloves garlic
– 1 dessertspoon oil
– salt, pepper
– 1 l (1¾ pt) Burgundy wine
– thyme, bay-leaves

Lard the beef with the fat bacon. Put the oil into a casserole dish and line the base with bacon rind. Over this, place the meat, peeled vegetables, two whole cloves of garlic, and mixed herbs (*bouquet garni*). Season with salt and pepper and pour in the wine. Place the lid on the casserole dish and cook in the oven at Mark 4, 350°F (180°C) for 3½ hours.

Suggested wines:

Burgundy, Pommard, Beaujolais, Brouilly

Tournedos à la crème

Tournedos steaks with cream sauce

For 4 servings:

– 4 tournedos steaks (fillet)
– 25 g (1 oz) butter
– 100 g (3½ oz) mushrooms
– 1 truffle
– ½ teaspoon Armagnac
– 4 slices goose liver pâté
– salt, pepper
– crumbly bread
– 50 g (1½ fl oz) double cream

Fry the steaks in butter on both sides over a fierce heat. Remove from the pan and keep warm. Brown the chopped mushrooms for ten minutes in the resulting juices. Add the Armagnac to make a sauce. Now, add the chopped truffle and thicken with cream. Season the sauce with salt and pepper.
In each plate, arrange a steak on a slice of toasted bread. Place a slice of liver pâté on top of each steak and coat with the cream sauce.
Serve small buttered carrots as an accompaniment.

Suggested wines:

Bordeaux, Médoc

Veau au paprika
Paprika veal

For 6 servings:

– 1.5 kg (3 lb 4 oz) veal
– 2 tomatoes
– 2 medium sized onions
– $\frac{1}{4}$ l ($\frac{1}{2}$ pt) stock
– 1 dessertspoon plain flour
– 1 dessertspoon paprika
– salt, pepper
– juice of $\frac{1}{2}$ lemon
– 50 g (1$\frac{1}{2}$ fl oz) double cream
– oil

Gently fry pieces of veal in a little oil. Meanwhile peel the onions and tomatoes. Chop the onions and pulp the tomatoes. When the veal is well browned, sprinkle the flour over and stir well to blend. Moisten with the stock and add tomatoes, onions, salt, pepper and paprika. Cover and cook for 1$\frac{1}{2}$ hours on a low flame.
Just before serving, add the juice of half a lemon and the cream.
Serve with noodles.

Suggested wine:

A light red wine

Escalopes de veau à la crème
Veal escalopes with cream sauce

For 4 servings:

– 4 escalopes veal
– 1 dessertspoon butter
– 1 dessertspoon oil
– 150 g (4$\frac{1}{2}$ fl oz) double cream
– salt, pepper

Season the escalopes with salt and pepper. Heat the oil and butter in a frying pan and cook the escalopes over a medium heat. When they are crisp and golden, remove and keep hot.
Pour the cream into the pan and, using a fork, blend together with the meat juices. Bring this sauce to the boil and spoon immediately over the escalopes.
Serve with pasta. This can also be served with Chanterelle mushrooms.

Suggested wines:

Anjou, Vouvray, Saumur, Passe-tout-grain, Beaujolais

Escalopes panées
Veal escalopes in breadcrumbs

For 4 servings:

- 4 escalopes veal
- salt, pepper
- 2 tablespoons plain flour
- 2 eggs
- 100 g (3½ oz) dried breadcrumbs
- 1 lemon
- 50 g (2 oz) butter

Season the escalopes with salt and pepper. Roll in flour, dip in beaten egg, and then coat with breadcrumbs. Cook with butter in a frying pan. Serve with lemon wedges.

Suggested wine:

Light red wine

Paupiettes de veau
Veal olives

For 6 servings:

- 6 escalopes veal
- 300 g (12 oz) minced pork
- thyme, bay-leaves
- 1 tablespoon parsley
- salt, pepper
- 200 g (6 fl oz) double cream
- 300 g (11 oz) mushrooms
- butter

Ask your butcher to slice the escalopes very thinly. Lay this veal out flat and season with salt and pepper. Mix the minced pork with thyme, bay-leaves and chopped parsley, and spread over the slices of veal. Roll up and tuck in the ends to prevent the stuffing from escaping, and tie securely with string. Lightly brown with butter in a casserole dish, cover, and cook for 45 minutes on a low flame. Remove the veal olives from the dish and keep hot. Fry the mushrooms with salt and pepper in the remaining juices. When cooked, thicken the sauce with cream. Serve the veal olives covered with this mushroom sauce.

Suggested wine:

Light red wine

Veau marengo

Veal stewed with wine and tomatoes

For 6 servings:

– 1.5 kg (3 lb 4 oz) shoulder
  or breast of veal
– 500 g (1 lb 2 oz) tomatoes
– 150 g (5 oz) mushrooms
– 4 large onions
– 1 glass white wine
– 1 clove garlic
– salt, pepper
– thyme, bay-leaves
– 50 g (2 oz) butter
– 1 tablespoon plain flour

Cut the meat into pieces and fry in a casserole dish with a little butter. When they are well browned, sprinkle with flour and stir briskly. Add the chopped garlic, sliced onions, skinned and chopped tomatoes, thyme, bay-leaves, salt and pepper. Moisten with white wine and about 2 glasses of water or stock.

Cover and cook on a low heat for 1½ hours. Then add the mushrooms, prepared and cleaned, but not washed. Cook for a further 15 minutes and serve with creamed potatoes or pasta.

Suggested wines:

Pomerol, Brouilly

Blanquette de veau

Veal stew

For 6 servings:

– 1 kg (2 lb 2 oz) veal
  (breast, shoulder, rib)
– 150 g (5 oz) smoked bacon
– 6 carrots
– 3 medium sized onions
– 150 g (5 oz) mushrooms
– 2 dessertspoons oil or butter
– salt, pepper
– juice of ½ lemon
– 2 egg yolks
– 50 g (1½ fl oz) double cream
– 2 dessertspoons plain flour
– thyme, bay-leaves

Put the oil or butter into a casserole dish. Add the meat, cut into pieces, and the finely diced bacon. Fry the veal until browned on all sides. Meanwhile, peel the onions, carrots and mushrooms. Add to the well-browned meat. Season with salt, pepper, thyme and bay-leaves. Pour in enough water to cover the meat. Cover the casserole dish and cook for an hour. When cooked, remove the thyme and bay-leaves. Drain the vegetables and meat and reserve the cooking liquor. Reduce a little. Prepare a *roux* with the flour and butter and stir in the cooking liquor. Just before serving, add the lemon juice and the egg yolks blended with cream. Coat the meat and vegetables with this sauce and serve with rice or pasta.

Suggested wines:

Volnay, Vosne, Romanée, Médoc, Saint-Emilion

Épaule de veau farcie à l'oeuf
Shoulder of veal stuffed with eggs

For 6 servings:

- 1 shoulder veal
- 3 eggs
- 100 g (3½ oz) crumbly bread
- 1 glass stock
- 1 cup chopped parsley
- 1 dessertspoon lard
- salt, pepper
- 75 g (3 oz) butter

Bone the shoulder of veal. Season the inside with salt and pepper. Hard-boil the eggs. Crumble the bread and soak in the stock. Add salt, pepper, lard and chopped parsley, and mix well. Chop two hard-boiled eggs and add to the stuffing. Stuff the shoulder, placing the third egg whole into the middle of the stuffing. Carefully sew up the shoulder, and cook with butter in a casserole dish over a medium flame. Baste occasionally with water or stock.
This dish may also be cooked in the oven.

Jarret de veau au citron
Stewed knuckle of veal with lemon

For 4 servings:

- 2 knuckles veal
- 2 onions
- 5 tomatoes
- 5 carrots
- stick celery
- 3 lemons
- salt, pepper
- bay-leaves
- ¼ l (½ pt) white wine
- 50 g (2 oz) butter

Melt the butter in a casserole dish. Add the meat together with the onions, carrots cut into rounds, and chopped stick of celery. Allow to colour until the veal is well browned. Then add the skinned tomatoes, salt, pepper, bay-leaves, and the zest of a well-washed lemon. Moisten with the white wine and a glass of water. Cover and cook for 1 hour. Remove the meat and vegetables from the casserole with a skimmer. Arrange in a dish and keep hot.
Add the juice of 3 lemons to the cooking liquor.
Bring to the boil and spoon this sauce over the meat. Serve with rice.

Longe d'agneau aux herbes
Loin of lamb with herbs

For 4 servings:

- 1 loin lamb (8 chops)
- thyme
- bay-leaves
- rosemary
- 25 g (1 oz) butter
- salt, pepper

Chop the herbs. Season the meat with salt and pepper and then spread with butter. Sprinkle the herbs over all sides of the meat. Roast in an oven, turning frequently. Serve with fried potato balls and tomato halves stuffed with breadcrumbs and garlic (*Tomates provençales*).

Suggested wines:

Beaujolais, Côtes du Rhône

Côtes d'agneau à la tomate - *Provence*
Lamb chops with tomatoes

For 4 servings:

- 4 lamb chops
- 4 tomatoes
- 2 shallots
- 2 cloves garlic
- 1 bay-leaf
- salt, pepper
- 50 g (2 oz) butter
- 50 g (2 oz) olives
- 2 tablespoons oil

Melt the butter in a saucepan. Add the chopped shallots and fry lightly. Add the tomatoes, skinned and roughly chopped, crushed garlic, bay-leaf, salt and pepper. Simmer gently until the tomatoes are completely reduced to a pulp. Now season the lamb chops with salt and pepper, and toss in oil in a frying pan.
When the chops are well browned, serve with the tomato sauce and garnish with olives.

Suggested wines:

Rosé Provençale, Rosé Corse

Gigot en croûte

Leg of lamb in a pastry crust

For 8 servings:

- 1 leg lamb (or mutton) (2-3 kg (4.5-6.5 lb))
- 1 kg (2 lb) sausage meat with herbs
- 6 cloves garlic
- thyme
- 50 g (2 oz) butter
- 600 g (1 lb 8 oz) short pastry
- 1 egg
- salt, pepper

Rub the lamb with garlic, add salt and pepper, spread with butter, and cook in the oven. After 45 minutes, remove from the oven and reserve the skimmed meat juices. Prepare the short pastry and roll out half on a pastry board. Mix the thyme with a little pepper into the sausage meat. Spread half the sausage meat flat over the pastry. Place the warmed leg of lamb on top and cover with the rest of the sausage meat. Roll out the rest of the pastry to cover the meat. Seal the edges tightly and decorate with leaf-shaped pieces of pastry. Make a vent in the top of the pastry, and glaze with egg. Cook for a further hour in a moderate oven, Mark 4, 350°F (180°C), covering the pastry crust with buttered paper to prevent from browning too quickly.
Serve with French beans and *pommes dauphine.*
The French beans may be heated in the reserved meat juices from the leg of lamb.

Suggested wine:

Red Burgundy

Gigot en braillouse - *Charente-Poitou*

Leg of lamb with potatoes

For 6 servings:

- 1 small leg lamb or mutton (2 kg (4.5 lb))
- 4 cloves garlic
- 1 slice larding bacon
- 1.5 kg (3 lb 4 oz) potatoes
- salt, pepper

The name of this recipe derives from the dialect of Charente and literally means 'Weeping leg of lamb'.
Peel and slice the potatoes. Cover the base of a large casserole dish with the slice of larding bacon. Over this spread the potato slices, seasoned with salt and pepper. Press halves of peeled garlic cloves into the leg of lamb. Place the leg of lamb prepared in this way on top of the potato slices. Cover the casserole dish and cook in a moderate oven Mark 4, 350°F (180°C) for 2 hours, without removing the lid. While the lamb is being braised, the potatoes soak up, and are cooked in, the meat juices. At the end of the cooking time, turn off the oven, but leave the meat in until ready to serve. Serve straight from the casserole dish.

Suggested wines:

Red Bordeaux or Burgundy

Brochettes d'agneau
Skewered lamb

For 4 servings:

– **500 g (1 lb 2 oz) lamb**
– **salt, pepper**
– **oil**
– **thyme**

Cut the lamb into cubes. Add salt and pepper. Impale the pieces of meat on skewers. Sprinkle with sprigged thyme and brush each side of the skewers with oil. Cook under grill or over charcoal. Take care to cook slowly, and if necessary brush with a little more oil to prevent the meat from drying out.

Suggested wines:

Saint-Emilion, Pommard, Nuits-Saint-Georges, Médoc, Beaujolais

Cassoulet
Bean stew

For 6 servings:

– **1 kg (2 lb 2 oz) dried haricot beans**
– **2 carrots**
– **2 onions**
– **3 cloves garlic**
– **3 tomatoes**
– **salt, pepper**
– **500 g (1 lb 2 oz) preserved goose**
  (or a shoulder of lamb)
– **250 g (9 oz) breast mutton**
– **1 garlic sausage**
– **200 g (7 oz) streaky bacon**
– **1 slice larding bacon**
– **breadcrumbs**

Soak the beans overnight. Line the base of a casserole dish or earthenware terrine with the larding bacon. Over this, place half the well-drained beans, seasoned with salt and pepper. Add the onions, roughly chopped, and all the meats cut into pieces. Cover with the rest of the beans. Pulp the tomatoes and mix with chopped garlic, salt and pepper. Pour this tomato purée over the beans, sprinkle with breadcrumbs, and spread with goose or other fat. Cook in the oven Mark 4, 350°F (180°C) for 2 hours.
Serve straight from the cooking dish.

Suggested wines:

Cahors, Madiran

Jambon à la crème
Ham in cream sauce

For 6 servings:

– 6 thick slices Bayonne ham
  (or mild gammon)
– 2 glasses Muscat de Frontignan
  wine
– $\frac{1}{4}$ l ($\frac{1}{2}$ pt) double cream
– salt, pepper

Arrange the slices of ham to overlap in a large, shallow pan. Moisten with the Muscat wine. Season with salt and pepper. Cook very gently for 45 minutes.
Then remove the ham and keep hot.
Reduce the cooking liquor and thicken with cream just before serving. Serve with spinach and boiled potatoes.

Suggested wines:

Chablis, Sancerre, Brouilly

Palette fumée aux lentilles
Smoked shoulder of pork with lentils

For 6 servings:

– 1 smoked shoulder pork
  (about 1.5 kg (3 lb 4 oz))
– 500 g (1 lb 2 oz) lentils
– 4 carrots
– 3 medium sized onions
– thyme and bay-leaves
– salt and pepper
– 2 cloves

Soak the lentils for 1 hour. Cover with water and cook in a saucepan. Add the thyme, bay-leaves, carrots, onions spiked with cloves, salt and pepper. Cook for 45 minutes. In another saucepan, cook the shoulder of pork in plenty of water. After 45 minutes, remove and drain. Add the meat to the lentils and continue cooking on a low flame. When cooked, the lentils should have absorbed nearly all the water.

Suggested wines:

Morgon, Bourgueil

Andouillettes grillées - *Ile-de-France*
Grilled chitterling sausages

For 4 servings:

– 4 chitterling sausages
– salt, pepper

Prick each sausage with the point of a knife to prevent from bursting when heated. Season the sausage with salt and pepper and cook under a grill or over charcoal. Turn frequently so that all sides are well cooked. Serve with mustard and a side dish of chipped potatoes or fried potato balls.

Suggested wines:

Chablis, Red Bordeaux

Tripes à la mode de Caen - *Normandie*
Braised tripe

For 4 servings:

– 600 g (1 lb 5 oz) tripe
– 60 g (2 oz) butter
– 3 medium sized carrots
– 3 medium sized onions
– 2 cloves garlic
– 2 cloves
– Pinch thyme
– 2 bay-leaves
– 1 tablespoon parsley
– 100 g (3½ oz) smoked back bacon rashers
– 1 calf's foot (or pig's trotter)
– 200 g (7 oz) streaky bacon
– salt, pepper
– small bottle dry white wine

Wash the tripe thoroughly in plenty of water. Put the butter into a 4-pint flameproof casserole dish and fry the peeled and diced carrots, sliced onions and diced smoked bacon until golden-brown. Add crushed garlic, cloves, thyme, bay-leaves and chopped parsley. Cut the calf's foot (or pig's trotter) in half lengthways. Cut the tripe into 1 inch cubes, blanch in boiling water, drain and add both to the casserole dish. Pour on white wine and cover with slices of streaky bacon. Tightly close the lid of the casserole dish and cook for about 7 hours.
Remove calf's foot (or pig's trotter); sprinkle with chopped parsley and serve very hot.

Suggested drinks:

Cider, Muscadet

Rognons à la crème

Kidneys in cream sauce

For 4 servings:

- 4 veal kidneys
- 25 g (1 oz) butter
- 50 g (1½ fl oz) double cream
- 1 tablespoon port
- 1 large pinch corn flour
- salt, pepper

Season the kidneys with salt and pepper, and brown with butter in a casserole dish. Cook gently without covering. When the kidneys are cooked, take the casserole off the heat and skim the fat from the pan juices. Cut the kidneys into thin strips and return to the casserole dish. Blend the cornflour with the cream and add the port. Thicken the meat juices with this cream. Adjust the seasoning, gently reheat, and serve as soon as the sauce starts to boil.

Suggested wines:

Côte de Beaune, Médoc

Boudin aux pommes - *Normandie*

Black pudding with apples

For 4 servings:

- 4 small black puddings
- 1 kg (2 lb 2 oz) cooking apples
- 100 g (3½ oz) butter
- salt, pepper

Peel and quarter the apples. Place the apples with 2½ oz of butter in a frying pan and gently brown. Season the black puddings with salt and pepper and fry in another pan with the remaining butter.
The puddings should be well cooked. The apples should be turned gently during cooking so they do not disintegrate.
Serve the puddings and apples together.

Suggested drinks:

Cider, Bourgueil, Beaujolais

6
Salads

Salade frisée à l'ail
Endive with garlic

For 4 servings:

- 1 endive
- 2 tablespoons oil
- 1 tablespoon vinegar
- salt, pepper
- 2 cloves garlic
- 150 g (5 oz) plain flour
- 200 g (7 oz) butter
- 150 g (5 oz) anchovies
- 1 egg

Prepare a short pastry with the flour and butter. Add salt, a chopped clove of garlic and season well with pepper. Spread this pastry out onto a buttered baking sheet. Cover half with a purée prepared from anchovies mixed with a little butter. Fold the pastry to overlap, glaze with egg, and cook in the oven. When cooked, cut into squares. Now wash the lettuce, drain well, and put into a salad bowl. Prepare an oil and vinegar dressing (*vinaigrette*), season with salt and pepper, and add a crushed clove of garlic.
Toss the lettuce in the dressing just before serving with the anchovy squares.

Salade de pissenlits au lard
Dandelion salad with bacon

For 4 servings:

- 250 g (9 oz) dandelion leaves
- 150 g (5 oz) smoked bacon
- salt, pepper
- 2 tablespoons oil
- 1 tablespoon vinegar
- 2 eggs (optional)

Wash and pick over the dandelion leaves. Remove the large, tough leaves and keep only the hearts. Drain this salad well and place in a salad bowl. Chop the bacon into small pieces and brown in a pan with a spoonful of oil. When crisp, add two spoonfuls of vinegar, some salt and pepper, and a spoonful of oil. Pour this dressing over the dandelion leaves while still hot. Two sliced hard-boiled eggs can be added if desired.

Suggested wine:

Beaujolais

Salade niçoise
Salad niçoise

For 4 servings:

– 6 tomatoes
– 6 eggs
– 8 anchovy fillets
– 2 sweet peppers
– 2 slices ham
– 100 g (3½ oz) olives
– salt, pepper
– 3 tablespoons oil, 1 tablespoon vinegar

Hard-boil the eggs and allow to cool. Peel and cut into quarters. In a dish arrange quarters of tomato and egg, finely chopped peppers, pieces of diced ham, and black and green olives.
Prepare a well seasoned *vinaigrette*.
Pour this dressing over the salad just before serving. When in season, add fresh French beans, which have been cooked and cooled, to the above ingredients.

Salade de cervelas - *Alsace*
Cervelat salad

For 4 servings:

– 3 cervelat sausages
– 2 shallots
– 2 tablespoons oil, 1 tablespoon vinegar
– 1 egg
– salt, pepper
– 2 tablespoons chopped parsley

Hard-boil the egg and allow to cool. Remove the shell and separate the white from the yolk.
Cut the cervelat sausages into thin slices and place in a salad bowl. Chop the shallots.
Prepare a dressing with salt, pepper, oil, vinegar and the mashed egg yolk. Add the shallots and chopped parsley to the dressing. Mix with the cervelats.
It is best to add the dressing to the cervelats in advance, whereas with green salads it is added just before serving.

Salade de pois chiches
Chick-pea salad

For 4 servings:

– **500 g (1 lb 2 oz) cooked chick-peas**
– **2 eggs**
– **2 tomatoes**
– **2 shallots**
– **1 tablespoon parsley**
– **salt, pepper**
– **3 tablespoons oil, 1 tablespoon vinegar**

Having cooked the chick-peas, allow to cool, and place in a dish. Quarter the tomatoes and hard-boil the eggs. Arrange quarters of tomato and egg around the dish. Chop the shallots and parsley, and add to a *vinaigrette* seasoned with salt and pepper.
Pour this dressing over the chick-peas.

Salade de boeuf
Beef salad

For 4 servings:

– **400 g (1 lb) cold boiled beef**
– **2 tomatoes**
– **2 boiled potatoes**
– **12 gherkins**
– **2 shallots**
– **1 clove of garlic**
– **salt, pepper**
– **2 tablespoons oil, 1 tablespoon vinegar**
– **parsley**
– **mustard**

Use the left-overs from meat cooked in a stock pot. Remove both the fat and the tendons. Cut the meat into small cubes. Take two potatoes boiled in their jackets; peel, and cut into pieces.
Mix the meat with the potatoes, quarters of tomato, and slices of gherkin.
Make a dressing with oil, vinegar, salt, pepper and a little mustard. Add a clove of garlic and some parsley, both chopped.
Just before serving, pour this dressing over the salad.

Salade d'endives aux noix
Chicory salad with nuts

For 4 servings:

- 500 g (1 lb 2 oz) chicory
- 100 g (3½ oz) Gruyère cheese
- 20 walnuts
- 2 tablespoons meat stock
- salt, pepper
- 2 tablespoons oil, 1 tablespoon vinegar

Wash the chicory and remove the outer leaves. Crack the walnuts. Cut the Gruyère into small cubes.
Prepare a *vinaigrette* with salt, pepper, oil and vinegar, and add the lean meat stock.
Pour this dressing over the salad and serve.

Salade de betteraves à la crème
Beetroot salad in cream sauce

For 6 servings:

- 700 g (1 lb 9 oz) beetroot
- 50 g (1½ fl oz) double cream
- juice of ½ lemon
- 1 teaspoon mustard
- salt, pepper
- parsley, chives

Cook the beetroot, either in salted water or in the oven. Leave to cool, then peel and cut the beetroot into small cubes. Prepare a sauce by blending the cream with the lemon juice and mustard. Season with salt, pepper and chopped herbs.
Turn the beetroot in this sauce before serving.

Salade de poivrons
Pepper salad

For 6 servings:

– 2 red peppers
– 2 yellow peppers
– 2 sticks celery
– 4 gherkins
– 3 carrots
– 1 chilli pepper
– 12 spring onions
– salt, pepper
– 1 glass oil
– 2 glasses white wine
– juice of 1 lemon
– 1 tablespoon parsley

Peel and cut all the vegetables into small pieces. Put the oil into a casserole dish. Toss in the vegetables and cook for 10 minutes. Then add the white wine, lemon juice, and chopped parsley. Season with salt and pepper, and braise over a low flame for 30 minutes more.
Serve well chilled.

Salade céleri et pommes
Celery and apple salad

For 4 servings:

– 1 celery
– 2 apples
– 200 g (7 oz) Mimolette cheese or hard cheddar
– 20 walnuts
– salt, pepper
– 2 tablespoons oil
– 1 tablespoon vinegar or lemon juice

Wash and prepare the celery. Cut the celery sticks and apples into pieces. Prepare the nuts. Cut the cheese into cubes.
Make a dressing by blending together salt, pepper, oil, and vinegar. The vinegar can be replaced by lemon juice.
Mix the ingredients in a salad bowl and pour the dressing over just before serving.

Salade de champignons crus

Raw mushroom salad

For 4 servings:

- 250 g (10 oz) field mushrooms
- 1 lemon
- 2 tablespoons olive oil
- salt, pepper
- 1 dessertspoon parsley

Wash and rub the mushrooms. Dry immediately in a cloth, and slice.
Prepare a dressing with olive oil, lemon juice, salt and pepper. Add a little chopped parsley.
Toss the mushrooms in the dressing and leave for one hour before serving. To prevent the mushrooms from turning brown, squeeze lemon juice over.

Salade de chou rouge

Red cabbage salad

For 6 servings:

- ½ red cabbage
- 100 g (3½ oz) dry white cheese
- chives
- salt, pepper
- 2 tablespoons oil, 1 tablespoon vinegar

Discard the outer leaves and cut out the hard stalk before shredding the red cabbage.
Prepare a well seasoned vinegar and oil dressing (*vinaigrette*), and add a good amount of chopped chives. Mix the shredded red cabbage with the crumbled white cheese and add the dressing.

Salade de lentilles

Lentil salad

For 6 servings:

- 500 g (1 lb 2 oz) lentils
- 3 medium sized onions
- 3 medium sized carrots
- thyme, bay-leaves
- parsley
- salt, pepper
- 3 tablespoons oil,
  1 tablespoon vinegar
- garlic
- mustard

Soak the lentils overnight. Then cook in water with the onions, carrots, a clove of garlic, mixed herbs, salt and pepper. When cooked, drain and leave to cool. Cut the carrots into slices and remove the thyme and bay-leaves.
Prepare a dressing with a small teaspoon of strong mustard, salt, pepper, oil, vinegar and chopped parsley. Mix this dressing with the lentils well before serving.

7
Poultry

Poule au pot
Boiled chicken in broth

For 4 servings:

- 1.8 kg (3 lb 8 oz) chicken
- 2 carrots
- 2 leeks
- 3 medium sized onions
- 3 turnips
- 1 stick celery
- bouquet garni
- salt, pepper
- gherkins

Roast one of the onions in the oven, taking care not to burn.
Meanwhile, truss and put the chicken in salted cold water and cook. When the water boils, skim and add the peeled vegetables, mixed herbs and roast onion. Season with salt and pepper and cook over a low heat for 1½ hours. Partially cover, to allow a little of the cooking water to evaporate and make the broth stronger. When cooked, remove the mixed herbs and roast onion.
Serve the chicken and the vegetables together and the broth separately. Garnish with gherkins.

Poulet quarante gousses d'ail
Chicken with forty cloves of garlic

For 4 servings:

- 1 large drawn chicken
- 40 cloves garlic
- salt
- farmhouse loaf
- 3 tablespoons olive oil
- bay-leaves, thyme

Season the inside of the chicken with salt, stuff with thyme and bay-leaves, and truss.
Place the chicken in an earthenware or cast-iron casserole dish and surround with all 40 unpeeled garlic cloves. Pour several dessertspoons of oil over the chicken. Cover and cook in the oven for 1½ hours at Mark 4, 350°F (180°C).
Meanwhile, toast some slices of farmhouse loaf.
Serve the chicken straight from the casserole dish.
Spread the toast with the braised peeled garlic to eat with the chicken. Those people who neither like the smell nor the taste of garlic will be surprised at the delicate flavour imparted by this dish, as the garlic cooked in its skin is not at all strong.

Suggested wines:

Beaujolais, Médoc

Poulet basquaise

Chicken basque

For 4 servings:

- 1 chicken
- 4 tomatoes
- 4 green peppers
- 2 dessertspoons plain flour
- 100 g (3½ oz) Bayonne ham
  (or mild gammon)
- 1 glass white wine
- 3 dessertspoons goose or
  chicken fat
- 1 shallot

Cut the chicken into serving pieces, coat in flour, and season with salt and pepper. Melt the fat in a casserole dish and place the chicken pieces in to brown. Now skin and pulp the tomatoes; peel and chop the shallots; and peel and slice the peppers into strips. Cut the ham into small cubes.

When the chicken is golden-brown, add the tomatoes, shallots, strips of peppers and cubes of ham, then moisten with white wine. Cover and cook over a low heat for 30 minutes.

Pour the juices over the chicken.

Serve with rice, pasta or boiled potatoes.

Suggested wines:

Madiran, Red Bordeaux

Poulet frit

Fried chicken

For 4 servings:

- 1 chicken
- thyme, bay-leaves
- salt, pepper
- 2 eggs
- 50 g (2 oz) flour
- 200 g (7 oz) dried breadcrumbs
- cooking oil

Cut the chicken into serving pieces. Strip the thyme and chop the bay-leaves. Season the chicken pieces with salt and pepper and sprinkle with thyme and chopped bay-leaves. Roll in flour, then dip in the beaten egg and coat in breadcrumbs. Fry in a deep fryer and remove with a skimmer as soon as the chicken is crisp and golden.

Serve with creamed potatoes or fresh spring vegetables (green peas, French beans, new carrots).

This dish is very quick to make and is ideal for those who want a carefully prepared meal, but have little time to spare.

Suggested wines:

Brouilly, Juliénas, Mercurey

Poulet au champagne
Chicken with champagne

For 4 servings:

– 1 chicken
– 150 g (5 oz) button mushrooms
– 1 tomato
– 50 g (2 oz) butter
– salt, pepper
– 2 dessertspoons brandy
– 100 g (3 fl oz) fresh double cream
– ½ bottle champagne
– 1 teaspoon plain flour

Cut the chicken into serving pieces. Brown with butter in a casserole dish. Season with salt and pepper. When the pieces are golden-brown, dust with flour and flame with brandy. Then add the skinned, pulped tomato and the peeled button mushrooms. Pour in the champagne. Cover and cook for 20 minutes. Thicken the sauce with cream just before serving.
To ensure the success of this dish, choose a good champagne which is not too sour, and a very ripe tomato; otherwise, the acidity of both could prove disastrous.

Suggested wine:

Champagne

Poulet aux morilles
Chicken with morels

For 4 servings:

– 1 chicken
– 300 g (11 oz) morel mushrooms
– 50 g (2 oz) butter
– salt, pepper
– 1 dessertspoon plain flour
– 150 g (4½ fl oz) double cream

Cut the chicken into serving pieces. Melt the butter in a shallow pan and place the chicken in to fry. When the chicken pieces are well browned on all sides add salt and pepper. Sprinkle with flour and stir well. Moisten with a glass of stock or water. Add the morels. Cover and cook for 20 minutes. Just before serving, thicken the cooking liquor with cream.

Poulet aux champignons

Chicken with mushrooms

For 4 servings:

- **1.5 kg (3 lb 4 oz) chicken**
- **300 g (11 oz) cultivated mushrooms**
- **½ l (1 pt) dry white wine (Chablis)**
- **50 g (2 oz) butter**
- **2 medium sized onions**
- **2 egg yolks**
- **50 g (1½ fl oz) fresh double cream**
- **salt, pepper**
- **bouquet garni**
- **1 dessertspoon plain flour**
- **2 tablespoons brandy**

Melt the butter in a casserole dish to fry the pieces of chicken. When the chicken is golden-brown, sprinkle with flour and flame with brandy. Add salt, pepper, mixed herbs and mushrooms. Slice and add the onions. Moisten with white wine and cook gently for an hour. Then thicken the sauce with cream and egg yolks blended together.
Serve immediately.

Suggested wine:

Chablis

Poulet sauté au curry

Sauté chicken in curry sauce

For 4 servings:

- **1.5 kg (3 lb 4 oz) chicken**
- **½ l (1 pt) vegetable or chicken stock**
- **50 g (2 oz) butter**
- **salt, pepper**
- **1 dessertspoon plain flour**
- **thyme**
- **1 teaspoon curry powder**
- **50 g (1½ fl oz) double cream**

Cut the chicken into pieces and brown with butter in a casserole dish. Add salt, pepper, sprigged thyme and curry powder. Pour in the stock, cover, and cook for 45 minutes. Remove the chicken pieces and reduce the cooking liquor to half. Thicken this reduced liquor with a dessertspoon of flour; reboil, then add the cream. Return the chicken pieces to the sauce and serve very hot with curried rice.

Coq en pâte

Chicken in a pastry crust

For 5 servings:

- 1.5 kg (3 lb 4 oz) chicken
- salt, pepper
- 25 g (1 oz) butter
- thyme, bay-leaves
- 400 g (14 oz) short pastry
- 1 egg yolk

Season the chicken with salt and pepper and spread liberally with butter. Cook in a hot oven Mark 6, 400°F (200°C). When the chicken is golden-brown, stuff with thyme and bay-leaves. Make an undercrust with the pastry, and place the chicken over, then cover with the rest of the pastry. A chicken head may also be shaped out of the pastry. Decorate, glaze with egg, and cook in the oven for 35 minutes. Carve hot at the table.
The flavour imparted to the chicken by the thyme and bay-leaves adds to the charm of this dish, so do not stint on the amount of herbs used.

Suggested wine:

Light red wine

Poulet à la crème

Chicken with cream sauce

For 4 servings:

- 1.5 kg (3 lb 4 oz) chicken
- 1 medium sized carrot
- 1 medium sized onion
- 2 dessertspoons plain flour
- 1 egg yolk
- 150 g (4½ fl oz) double cream
- salt, pepper
- ¼ l (½ pt) stock
- 50 g (2 oz) butter

Cut the chicken into serving pieces, and brown in a casserole dish with the carrot, onion and butter. When the chicken is golden-brown, dust with flour and stir with a wooden spoon. Season with salt and pepper and moisten with stock. Cover and cook for about 20 minutes over a low heat. Remove the pieces of chicken, strain the cooking liquor, and add the cream and egg yolk blended together. Serve the chicken pieces in a dish and coat with the sauce.

Suggested wines:

White wines: Beaujolais, Brouilly

Poulet aux girolles

Chicken with chanterelles

For 4 servings:

- 1.5 kg (3 lb 4 oz) chicken
- 300 g (11 oz) mushrooms,
  (preferably Chanterelles)
- 125 g (4½ oz) smoked bacon
- salt, pepper
- 1 shallot
- 50 g (2 oz) butter

Cut the chicken into pieces. Fry pieces of chopped bacon with butter in a casserole dish. Place the chicken pieces in and brown on all sides. Then add the chanterelles with salt and pepper. Chop the shallot and add to the chicken. Cover and cook for 20 minutes. Take care that the chicken does not stick to the casserole dish and, if necessary, add a few spoonfuls of water or stock.
The sauce should be very thick.
Serve with creamed potatoes.

Poulet à l'estragon

Chicken with tarragon

For 4 servings:

- 1.5 kg (3 lb 4 oz) chicken
- 50 g (2 oz) butter
- 2 dessertspoons oil
- 6 shallots
- tarragon
- salt, pepper
- 1 glass dry white wine
- 100 g (3 fl oz) double cream
- 2 egg yolks

Melt the butter and oil in a casserole dish and brown the pieces of chicken. Add the chopped shallots and fry for a little longer. Season with salt and pepper. Add 3 or 4 good sprigs of tarragon and white wine. Cover and cook over a low heat for 30 minutes. When cooked, remove the chicken from the casserole dish. Keep hot. Chop 2 sprigs of tarragon and add to the cream. Blend the cream with the egg yolks. Thicken the chicken stock with this mixture. Pour the sauce over the chicken and serve.

Poule au blanc

Chicken in white sauce

For 4 servings:

- 1.5 kg (3 lb 4 oz) chicken
- 2 carrots
- 1 leek
- 1 medium sized onion
- salt, pepper
- 75 g (3 oz) plain flour
- 3 egg yolks
- 100 g (3 fl oz) double cream
- 75 g (3 oz) butter

Peel and put the vegetables into a pot with 2 l (3½ pt) of water. Season with salt and pepper. Cook for 45 minutes. Prepare and truss the chicken. Cook in stock for about 45 minutes. When cooked, drain and keep hot. Slightly reduce the stock for at least 30 minutes. Prepare a bechamel-type sauce from the butter, flour and 1¼ pt cooled stock. Blend the egg yolks with the cream and add to the sauce just before serving. Arrange the chicken in a serving dish and pour this sauce over. Serve any remaining sauce in a sauce-boat.
This dish goes well with rice.

Suggested wines:

Light red Burgundy, Chablis, Mâcon

Dinde aux marrons

Turkey stuffed with chestnuts

For 8 servings:

- 3 kg (6 lb 6 oz) turkey
- 1 kg (2 lb 2 oz) chestnuts
- 400 g (14 oz) minced pork
- ½ glass brandy
- salt, pepper
- 50 g (2 oz) truffles
- 2 carrots
- 1 medium sized onion
- 50 g (2 oz) butter
- 1 basin stock

Peel and boil the chestnuts in water. When cooked, but still firm, remove the inner skins. Take a third of these chestnuts and blend with the minced pork. Add brandy, chopped truffles in their juice, salt and pepper. Fill the turkey with this stuffing and carefully sew up. Spread the turkey generously with butter and place on a large baking dish. Peel and slice the onion and carrots and arrange with the remaining chestnuts around the turkey in the dish. Moisten with the stock. Cook in the oven at Mark 4, 350°F (180°C) for 1½ hours, basting from time to time with the cooking liquor. Should the top of the turkey cook too quickly, it may be covered with a slice of larding bacon.
When cooked, strain the juices from the turkey and make a sauce by adding half a glass of white wine to the cooking residue.
Reheat the chestnuts left in the juices and serve with the turkey.

Suggested wines:

Pommard, Nuits-Saint-Georges, Châteauneuf-du-Pape

Poulet sauté au citron
Sauté chicken with lemon

For 4 servings:

– 1.5 kg (3 lb 4 oz) chicken
– 50 g (2 oz) butter
– 3 carrots
– 2 dessertspoons plain flour
– 1 medium sized onion
– $\frac{1}{4}$ l ($\frac{1}{2}$ pt) stock
– 2 lemons
– salt, pepper
– 1 bay-leaf

Melt the butter in a casserole dish.. Cut the chicken into joints and brown in the butter. Peel and slice the carrots and onions and add to the chicken. When browned, dust with flour and stir with a wooden spoon. Pour in the stock. Wash a lemon and grate the zest. Add this zest, together with the juice of the lemon and the bay-leaf. Cook over a low heat for 45 minutes. Just before serving, add the juice of the second lemon, check the seasoning, and serve.
The sauce should taste slightly acid and the chicken should melt in the mouth.

Suggested wines:

Brouilly, Chiroubles

Coq au vin - *Bourgogne-Bresse*
Chicken in red wine

For 8 servings:

– 1 young chicken
– 1 bottle red Burgundy wine
– 4 medium sized onions
– 100 g (3$\frac{1}{2}$ oz) button mushrooms
– 1 clove garlic
– thyme, bay-leaves
– 125 g (4$\frac{1}{2}$ oz) smoked bacon
– 1 dessertspoon plain flour
– 3 dessertspoons oil
– 2$\frac{}{}$ g (1 oz) butter
– brandy
– salt, pepper

Heat the oil and butter in a casserole dish. Peel the onions and cut the bacon into small cubes. Fry the sliced onions and bacon cubes in the casserole dish. Cut the chicken into pieces and brown in the casserole. Season with salt and pepper. When the chicken is golden-brown, flame with brandy and sprinkle with flour. Stir with a wooden spoon. Moisten with the wine. Add garlic, mushrooms, and mixed herbs (*bouquet garni*). Cover and cook for 20 minutes. Adjust the seasoning of the sauce and serve with boiled potatoes.

Suggested wines:

Morgon, Côte de Beaune

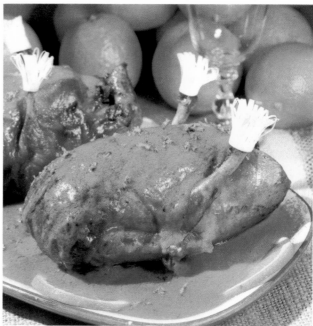

Pigeons aux raisins

Pigeons with grapes

For 4 servings:

- 4 pigeons
- 1 kg (2 lb 2 oz) Muscadine grapes
- 50 g (2 oz) butter
- salt, pepper
- 2 glasses white Alsatian wine
- slices larding bacon
- 2 tablespoons brandy

Bard the pigeons with the slices of bacon and fry with butter in a casserole dish. Brown well on all sides. Season with salt and pepper. Flame with brandy. Moisten with white wine, cover and cook for 20 minutes. After cooking for 10 minutes, remove the bacon slices and add the juice of 400 g (14 oz) of grapes. Finish cooking and add the remainder of the seeded grapes. Reduce for about 10 minutes.
Serve the pigeons surrounded with grapes and coated in the sauce.

Suggested wine:

Alsatian Muscat

Canard à l'orange

Duck with orange sauce

For 4 servings:

- 1 duck, 2 kg (4 lb)
- 2 medium sized carrots
- 1 medium sized onion
- thyme, bay-leaves
- 1 tomato
- salt, pepper
- 50 g (2 oz) butter
- 1 glass white wine
- 1 dessertspoon plain flour
- 6 oranges
- 6 sugar lumps
- $\frac{1}{2}$ glass wine vinegar

Fry the duck with butter in a casserole dish. When golden-brown on all sides, remove duck from the casserole dish and replace with sliced carrots, chopped onion, thyme, bay-leaves, tomato, salt and pepper. After 15 minutes, moisten with white wine and cook for a further 5 minutes. Then thicken with flour and replace the duck. Meanwhile, make a pale caramel by melting the sugar with a teaspoon of water on a hot flame. Add the vinegar and the juice from the oranges, with some of the chopped zest, and cook for a few minutes.
To serve, lay the duck on a dish and coat with the sauce, strained and blended with the caramel and orange mixture.

8
Game

Canard sauvage aux navets
Wild duck with turnips

For 4 servings:

– 1 duck, preferably wild
– 200 g (7 oz) butter
– 1.5 kg (3 lb 4 oz) young turnips
– thyme, bay-leaves
– 1 dessertspoon parsley
– salt, pepper
– 4 sugar lumps
– $\frac{1}{4}$ l ($\frac{1}{2}$ pt) stock
– 2 tablespoons plain flour
– 3 medium sized onions
– 2 tablespoons brandy

Brown the duck in a casserole dish with 100 g (4 oz) of butter. When golden-brown on all sides, season with salt and pepper and flame with brandy. Add thyme, bay-leaves and sliced onions. Moisten with the stock, cover, and cook for about 40 minutes. Meanwhile, put the remaining butter into a saucepan to braise the turnips. After 30 minutes, add the sugar and leave to brown. Thicken the cooking liquor with flour and serve the duck covered in the sauce, surrounded with turnips and sprinkled with parsley.

Suggested wines:

Pommard, Côte de Beaune, Red Bordeaux

Canard sauvage aux pommes
Wild duck with apples

For 4 servings:

– 1 duck, preferably wild
– 150 g (5 oz) butter
– 1 clove garlic
– thyme, 2 bay-leaves
– salt, pepper
– 1 dessertspoon powdered ginger
– 1 glass port
– 6 cooking apples
– redcurrant jelly

Put the butter into a casserole dish and brown the duck. When it is golden-brown on all sides, add the clove of garlic, thyme, bay-leaves, ginger, salt and pepper, and moisten with a small cup of water or stock. Cover and cook over a low heat for 40 minutes. Meanwhile, cook the peeled apples in the oven with a little butter. When the duck is cooked, lay in a serving dish and surround with the apples coated in redcurrant jelly.
Dilute the juices from the duck with port and spoon this sauce over the duck.

Suggested wines:

Vosne Romanée, Pomerol, Saint-Emilion

Faisan à la choucroute
Pheasant with sauerkraut

For 4 servings:

– 1 pheasant
– 1.5 kg (3 lb 4 oz) cooked sauerkraut
– 100 g (3½ oz) sliced smoked bacon
– 2 glasses dry white wine
– salt, pepper
– 50 g (2 oz) butter

Put the butter into a casserole dish and brown the pheasant, either whole or cut into serving pieces. When the pieces are golden-brown, remove from the casserole dish and line the base with slices of smoked bacon. On top place the sauerkraut and pieces of pheasant or whole pheasant, as the case may be.
Season with salt and pepper and moisten with the white wine.
Braise for 30 minutes.

Suggested wines:

Sylvaner, Riesling

Faisan en cocotte
Pheasant with mushrooms and onions

For 4 servings:

– 1 pheasant
– 50 g (2 oz) butter
– salt, pepper
– 16 button onions
– 300 g (11 oz) button mushrooms
– larding bacon

Prepare the pheasant and bard with the larding bacon. Truss well. Put the butter into a casserole dish and brown the pheasant on all sides. Season with salt and pepper and cover. Cook over a very gentle heat for 30 minutes. Meanwhile, prepare the button onions and mushrooms and place around the bird in the casserole dish. Continue cooking for a further 30 minutes. Serve the pheasant surrounded with the button onions and mushrooms.

Suggested wines:

Volnay, Vosne Romanée, Red Bordeaux or Burgundy

Faisan aux pommes

Pheasant with apples

For 4 servings:

– 1 pheasant
– larding bacon
– 200 g (7 oz) raisins
– 100 g (3½ oz) butter
– 6 cooking apples
– 1 glass port
– 150 g (5 oz) fine forcemeat
– salt, pepper
– 1 glass Calvados (apple brandy)

Stuff the pheasant with the fine forcemeat. Season with salt and pepper and brown in a casserole dish with 50 g (2 oz) of butter. Soak the raisins in the Calvados. Peel and cook the apples in the oven with the remaining butter and the port. Baste frequently, diluting the cooking liquor with a little water if necessary. During cooking, moisten with half a glass of water and add both the raisins and the Calvados.
Surround the pheasant with the apples and serve with the raisins and sauce.

Suggested wines:

Chambertin, Pommard, Red Burgundy or Bordeaux

Pigeon aux pommes

Pigeon with apples

For each serving:

– 1 pigeon
– 100 g (3½ oz) minced pork
– 25 g (1 oz) butter
– thyme
– salt, pepper
– 2 cooking apples
– 2 dessertspoons oil
– 1 dessertspoon brandy

Remove the leaves from the thyme and blend with the pork. Season with salt and pepper. Fill the pigeon with this stuffing and cook in a casserole dish with butter. Now peel and cut the apples into quarters and brown with oil in a frying pan. Turn the apples very carefully so as not to make a purée.
Stop cooking when the apples are still fairly firm. When the pigeon is cooked, flame with brandy and serve on a bed of apples. Coat with the juices from the pigeon.

Suggested wines:

Brouilly, Bourgueil, Pomerol

Perdreaux au chou

Partridge with cabbage

For 2 servings:

– 2 partridges
– 1 green cabbage
– 100 g (3½ oz) smoked bacon
– 1 Toulouse sausage or ½ lb good pork sausages
– 3 carrots
– 2 onions
– 1 glass dry white wine
– 25 g (1 oz) butter
– 2 tablespoons brandy
– salt, pepper
– larding bacon

Remove the outer leaves of the cabbage, blanch in boiling water for 15 minutes, and drain well. In a casserole dish, place the smoked bacon, cut into large pieces, and brown with the sliced onions and carrots. When everything is golden-brown, add the roughly chopped cabbage and the Toulouse sausage. Season with salt and pepper, and moisten with the white wine. Cover and cook over a very low heat for 1 hour. Bard the partridges with thin slices of larding bacon, cook in the oven for 45 minutes, and flame with brandy.
To serve, arrange the partridges on the bed of cabbage and pour the cooking liquor over.

Suggested wine:

Light red Burgundy

Perdrix à la choucroute

Partridge with sauerkraut

For 3 servings:

– 1 kg (2 lb 2 oz) raw sauerkraut
– 100 g (3½ oz) slices larding bacon
– ½ l (1 pt) dry white wine
– 50 g (2 oz) goose or chicken fat
– salt, pepper
– 300 g (11 oz) smoked bacon
– 1 smoked cooking sausage
– 3 barded partridges
– juniper berries

Line a casserole dish with the larding bacon. On top place the raw sauerkraut with the smoked sausage and bacon. Season with salt and pepper. Add juniper berries and moisten with the white wine. Cook in the oven Mark 4, 350°F (180°C) for 2½ hours. In a separate casserole dish, cook the partridges barded with thin slices of bacon in the goose fat for 30 minutes. Season with salt and pepper. After cooking the sauerkraut for 2½ hours, add the well-browned partridges with their cooking liquor. Return to the pan for 30 minutes. Serve everything together.

Suggested wines:

White Alsatian wine: Riesling, Sylvaner

Salmis de palombe - *Gascogne*

Ragoût of wood pigeon

For 4 servings:

– 2 wood pigeons
– 150 g (5 oz) ham
– 150 g (5 oz) mushrooms
– 4 shallots
– 2 medium sized onions
– 50 g (2 oz) butter
– salt, pepper
– 1 tablespoon plain flour
– 1 glass red wine
– 2 tablespoons brandy
– 1 tomato

Cut the wood pigeons in half and fry gently with butter in a casserole dish. When they are golden-brown, remove and add to the casserole the ham, mushrooms, shallots and onions, all finely chopped. Allow to brown. Then return the wood pigeons to the casserole dish, flame with brandy, and season with salt and pepper. Sprinkle with the flour, stir, and moisten with the red wine. Finally, add the skinned tomato. Cover and cook over a low heat for 45 minutes.

Suggested wines:

Pommard, Madiran

Civet de lièvre

Jugged hare

For 8 servings:

– 1 hare, 2 kg (4 lb 4 oz)
– ½ l (1 pt) Burgundy wine
– 250 g (9 oz) streaky bacon
– 50 g (2 oz) butter
– 200 g (7 oz) button onions
– thyme, bay leaves, parsley
– 2 cloves garlic
– 2 tablespoons plain flour
– salt, pepper
– 3 tablespoons brandy

Skin and cut the hare into pieces, reserving the blood to thicken the sauce. Brown these pieces with butter and diced bacon in a casserole dish. Add the button onions, salt and pepper. When the pieces of hare have coloured slightly, sprinkle with flour and leave to brown a little. Moisten with the red wine and add the mixed herbs and garlic. Cover and cook over a gentle heat until tender. Remove the pieces from the cooking liquor and thicken with the blood and brandy. Pass the sauce through a conical strainer, arrange the pieces of hare on a dish, and ladle the sauce over.
Alternatively, the sauce may be thickened by adding half a glass of cream to the hare's blood.
Serve with home-made noodles (p. 21) or boiled potatoes.

Suggested wine:

Morgon

Lapin à la moutarde
Rabbit with mustard

For 4 servings:

– 1 rabbit
– 100 g (3½ oz) fat bacon
– salt, pepper
– 50 g (2 oz) butter
– 1 glass strong mustard
– 150 g (4½ fl oz) fresh double cream
– bouquet garni
– 2 dessertspoons dry white wine

Lard the rabbit with fat bacon. Then cut into serving pieces and generously spread with mustard. Fry with butter in a shallow pan. When well browned, season with salt and pepper, moisten with 2 dessertspoons of white wine, and add the mixed herbs. Cover and cook on a low flame for 35 minutes.
Thicken the cooking liquor with cream just before serving.

Suggested wines:

Chablis, White Mâcon

Lapin sauté au lard
Sauté rabbit with bacon

For 4 servings:

– 1 rabbit
– 200 g (7 oz) smoked bacon
– 25 g (1 oz) butter
– salt, pepper
– thyme, 2 bay-leaves
– 1 cup stock

Cut the rabbit into serving pieces and the bacon into cubes. Fry both bacon and rabbit in a casserole dish with butter. When the rabbit is well browned, season with salt and pepper, add thyme and bay-leaves, and moisten with the stock. Cover and cook for 35 minutes over a low heat. If necessary, slightly reduce the cooking liquor before serving. Serve with pasta.

Suggested wines:

Mercurey, Saint-Amour, Côtes du Rhône

Lapin aux olives

Rabbit with olives

For 4 servings:

- 1 rabbit
- 200 g (7 oz) green olives
- 50 g (2 oz) butter
- 1 glass dry white wine
- 1 shallot
- 50 g (2 oz) smoked bacon
- salt, pepper

Cut the rabbit into serving pieces and fry in a casserole dish with the butter and thinly sliced bacon. Allow to colour for a further 15 minutes, stirring occasionally. The pieces of rabbit should be well browned. Then add the chopped shallot and the stoned olives. Moisten with the white wine and a glass of water. Season with salt and pepper, cover, and cook over a low flame for 40 minutes.

Lapin aux haricots

Rabbit with dried haricot beans

For 4 servings:

- 1 rabbit
- 4 medium sized onions
- 250 g (9 oz) smoked bacon
- 4 tomatoes
- 2 glasses dry white wine
- thyme, 1 bay-leaf
- salt, pepper
- 1 tablespoon oil
- 500 g (1 lb 2 oz) dried haricot beans

Soak the dried beans overnight. The following day, cook in water seasoned with salt and pepper. Meanwhile, dice the bacon and fry with oil in a casserole dish. Add the sliced onions, then the rabbit cut into pieces, and allow to brown. When the rabbit is well browned, add the pulped tomatoes, thyme and bay-leaves. Add salt and pepper and moisten with white wine. Cover and cook. After 30 minutes, add the drained beans, which should be cooked, but still firm. Simmer for 15 minutes and serve.
This dish may be prepared using fresh beans when in season which naturally require no soaking and are added to the rabbit with the tomatoes.

Suggested wines:

Cahors, Passe-tout-grains

Canard aux raisins verts
Duck with green grapes

For 4 servings:

– 1 duck
– 500 g (1 lb 2 oz) green grapes
– 50 g (2 oz) butter
– salt, pepper
– 2 tablespoons brandy

Gently fry the duck with butter in a casserole dish and brown well on all sides. Meanwhile squeeze the juice from half the grapes. When the duck is golden-brown, flame with brandy, season with salt and pepper, and add the grape juice. Cover and cook for 25 minutes. After cooking for 15 minutes, add the whole grapes and taste the cooking liquor. If it is too sour add a lump of sugar.
Serve the duck surrounded with grapes.

Selle de chevreuil
Saddle of venison

For 6 servings:

– 2 kg (4 lb 4 oz) saddle of venison
– 100 g (3½ oz) fat bacon
– 1 medium sized onion
– 1 carrot
– 2 glasses dry white wine
– 2 tablespoons oil
– peppercorns
– thyme, 2 bay-leaves
– 2 tablespoons parsley
– 50 g (2 oz) butter
– salt

Prepare a marinade using the onion, carrot, thyme, bay-leaves, salt, peppercorns, parsley and oil. Lard the saddle with fat bacon. Marinate the saddle for 24 hours, turning occasionally. Drain the saddle, spread with butter, and cook in an ovenproof dish. Surround with the ingredients from the marinade, and keep the liquid to one side. Cook in a hot oven at Mark 6, 400°F (200°C) for 60 minutes, and baste with the meat juices. The saddle should not be overcooked, as the flesh should remain pink in colour. When the saddle is ready, keep hot and add the liquid from the marinade to the meat juices. Reduce on a high heat.
Pour this sauce over the saddle and serve with chestnut purée and redcurrant jelly.

Suggested wine:

Full-bodied red Burgundy

9
Desserts

Figues fourrées

Stuffed figs

For 4 servings:

– **8 purple figs**
– **150 g (5 oz) almonds**
– **50 g (2 oz) caster sugar**
– **1 dessertspoon cream cheese**

Remove the skins from the almonds. Keeping 8 whole nuts to one side, reduce the rest to a powder. Add the sugar and cream cheese, and mix thoroughly to form a thick paste. Split the figs into quarters, taking care not to separate the pieces completely.

Open out the fig quarters and fill with a spoonful of the almond paste. Place a whole almond in the centre of each fig.

Tarte aux mûres

Mulberry tart

For 6 servings:

– **400 g (14 oz) short pastry**
– **1 kg (2 lb 2 oz) cooking apples**
– **50 g (2 oz) butter**
– **100 g (3½ oz) caster sugar**
– **200 g (7 oz) mulberries**

Line a flan ring with the pastry. Peel and slice the apples very thin. Fill the pastry with these apples. Sprinkle with sugar and place knobs of butter over.

Bake in a moderate oven. When cooked, allow to cool and garnish with mulberries.

Poires au vin
Pears in wine

For 8 servings:

- 8 cooking pears
- 1 l (1¾ pts) red wine
- 150 g (5 oz) caster sugar
- 2 sticks cinnamon
- ½ lemon
- 1 pinch cayenne pepper

Peel the pears whole, leaving the stalks intact. Poach in the red wine diluted with ½ litre (1 pint) of water to which the cinnamon sticks, the juice of half a lemon and the cayenne pepper have been added. When the pears are cooked, remove from the wine and keep in a cool place. Reduce the wine by half over a flame. Remove the cinnamon and add the sugar. Allow to cool and serve the pears in this syrup. For a novel version of this dish, replace the cinnamon by a few sprigs of fresh wild thyme.

Compote de poires caramélisée
Stewed pears in caramel

For 8 servings:

- 2 kg (4 lb 4 oz) pears
- 200 g (7 oz) caster sugar
- 150 g (5 oz) lump sugar
- ½ lemon

Peel and cut the pears into pieces. Cook the pears in a saucepan with a glass of water and the caster sugar. When they are cooked, strain through a sieve and pour into a deep dish. Add the juice of half a lemon and mix well. Now, prepare a caramel with a little water and the lump sugar. When the caramel is nice and brown, without being burnt, pour while still hot in round patterns over the stewed pears.
Serve immediately. For this recipe, a mixture of pears and apples can be used.

Poires en robe
Pears in their jackets

For 6 servings:

- 6 pears
- 150 g (5 oz) almonds
- 50 g (2 oz) sugar
- 2 egg yolks
- 500 g (1 lb 2 oz) puff pastry
- 1 egg for glazing

Choose fine ripe pears which are still firm. Prepare the puff pastry and roll out on the work surface. Chop the almonds and place in a mixing bowl. Add the sugar and egg yolks to the almonds. Work this paste well. Cut the puff pastry into large squares and place a whole pear on each. Surround with a little almond paste. Fold the pastry around to completely enclose the pears. Seal well. Glaze with egg and bake for 45 minutes in a moderate oven, Mark 4, 350°F (180°C). Serve warm or hot.

Tarte aux poires
Pear flan

For 4 servings:

- 500 g (1 lb 2 oz) short pastry
- 250 g (9 oz) cream cheese
- 50 g (1½ fl oz) double cream
- 4 pears
- 100 g (3½ oz) caster sugar
- 1 stick cinnamon
- raspberry jam

Prepare the short pastry and leave to rest. Meanwhile, peel and poach the pears in a syrup made with half the sugar and the cinnamon stick. Allow the pears to cool. The pastry should then be rolled out to line the flan ring. Bake in a moderate oven. When cooked, leave to cool and fill with some of the pears cut into pieces. Blend the cream cheese with the cream and the remainder of the sugar, and pour over the flan. Garnish with the remaining pieces of pear and coat with raspberry jam.

Gâteaux aux pêches et aux framboises
Peach and raspberry gâteau

For 6 servings:

- **125 g (5 oz) caster sugar**
- **100 g (4 oz) plain flour**
- **4 eggs**
- **pinch salt**
- **12½ g (½ oz) vanilla sugar**
- **⅛ l (¼ pt) custard cream filling**
- **4 peaches**
- **125 g (5 oz) raspberries**
- **100 g (3½ oz) butter**

Whisk the caster sugar and egg yolks together until pale and thick. Add the softened butter, flour, vanilla sugar and a small pinch of salt. Beat the egg whites until stiff and gently fold into the mixture.
Bake in a 17 cm (7 in) round, buttered cake tin in a moderate oven Mark 4, 350°F (180°C) for 30 minutes. Turn out immediately and leave to cool. Peel the peaches and poach in sugar syrup. When the sponge is cold, cut into 3 horizontal layers. Between each layer place peach slices, raspberries and a little custard cream filling.
The sponge may also be moistened with kirsch diluted in a little water.

Suggested wine:

Muscat de Frontignan

Tarte au fromage blanc
Cream cheese flan

For 6 servings:

- **300 g (11 oz) plain flour**
- **100 g (3½ oz) butter**
- **4 eggs**
- **2 tablespoons oil**
- **salt**
- **200 g (7 oz) cream cheese**
- **50 g (1½ fl oz) double cream**
- **150 g (5 oz) caster sugar**
- **1 orange**

Place the flour in a mixing bowl, make a hole in the centre and fill with two of the eggs, oil, butter, and a pinch of salt. Work these ingredients together adding a little water if necessary. Knead the dough well and roll into a ball. Leave to rest for 1 or 2 hours.
Butter a 10 in flan ring well and line with the rolled-out pastry. Blend together the cream cheese, cream, the two remaining eggs and sugar. Mix well and add the grated zest of an orange.
Fill the pastry case with this mixture and bake for about 1 hour in a moderate oven, Mark 4, 350°F (180°C). This is delicious hot or cold.

Oeufs à la neige
Snow eggs

For 4 servings:

- $\frac{1}{2}$ l (1 pt) milk
- 1 vanilla pod
- 4 eggs
- 100 g (3$\frac{1}{2}$ oz) caster sugar
- 100 g (3$\frac{1}{2}$ oz) icing sugar

Pour the milk into a large saucepan and add the vanilla pod. Heat gently until milk is hot but not boiling. Separate the whites from the yolks of the eggs. Whisk the yolks and caster sugar together until thick and creamy. Remove vanilla pod from milk, pour hot milk onto egg yolks whisking all the time. Heat the custard mixture until it just coats the back of a wooden spoon, do not boil as this will cause the custard to curdle. Pour the custard into a bowl and leave to cool. Whisk the egg whites until stiff, add half the icing sugar and whisk again until stiff. Fold in the remainder of the icing sugar. Poach spoonfuls of the meringue in simmering water. Turn the meringue after 5-6 minutes and poach other side. Remove from water and drain well. Arrange on the cold custard. The dish can be decorated by pouring pale caramel over the meringue.

Crème renversée
Caramel custard

For 6 servings:

- 1 l (1$\frac{3}{4}$ pt) milk
- 8 eggs
- 250 g (9 oz) caster sugar
- 2 vanilla pods
- 80 g (3 oz) lump sugar

Boil the milk and add the vanilla pods to infuse. Allow to cool. Cream together the eggs and caster sugar. Add the cooled milk to this mixture. Place the lump sugar in a saucepan with a spoonful of water. Heat until the sugar caramelizes. When it is light brown in colour, pour into a mould to coat the bottom and sides. Once the caramel has set, pour in the custard. Bake in a bain marie in a moderate oven, Mark 4, 350°F (180°C), for 45 minutes.
Turn out when completely cold.

Omelette à la confiture
Jam omelette

For 6 servings:

– **12 eggs**
– **½ glass rum**
– **50 g (2 oz) sugar**
– **pinch salt**
– **25 g (1 oz) butter**
– **jam: strawberry, cherry, peach,
  apricot, pear, etc.**

Beat the eggs and add a pinch of salt, the sugar, and rum. Put the butter into a frying pan, pour in the beaten eggs, and cook the omelette over a medium heat. When cooked, pour the jam into the centre of the omelette and fold over. Serve very hot.

Meringue glacée sauce chocolat
Ice cream meringue with chocolate sauce

For 8 servings:

– **16 meringue shells**
– **½ l (1 pt) vanilla ice cream**
– **100 g (3½ oz) cooking chocolate**
– **zest of orange**
– **25 g (1 oz) butter**

Prepare a chocolate sauce by meling the cooking chocolate with the butter and adding one or two spoonfuls of water. Add the orange zest and stir well to obtain a smooth cream. Allow to cool.
Place a large scoop of vanilla ice cream between two meringue shells for each guest. Pour over the chocolate sauce just before serving.

Beignets aux pommes

Apple fritters

For 6 servings:

- 1 kg (2 lb) apples
- 1 lemon
- 150 g (5 oz) plain flour
- 2 large eggs
- 2 fl oz milk
- 2½ fl oz beer
- 1 dessertspoon oil
- pinch of salt
- granulated sugar

Mix the flour, eggs and oil together in a bowl. Add the milk, beer and a pinch of salt. Blend all ingredients in a liquidizer. The batter must not be too thick. Leave to rest for a few hours. Peel, core and cut the apples into rings. Sprinkle these rings with lemon juice. Dip in batter and deep fry 2 or 3 rings at a time until golden. Dust with granulated sugar.
These fritters should be eaten straight out of the fryer!

Pommes au nid

Apples in the nest

For 6 servings:

- 6 small cooking apples
- 3-4 tablespoons lemon juice
- 3 eggs
- 150 g (5 oz) caster sugar
- pinch of salt
- 150 g (5 oz) self-raising flour
- 150 g (5 oz) butter
- grated rind of 1 lemon
- 6 glacé cherries

Peel and core the apples, toss each in the lemon juice. Stand apples in a well greased ovenproof dish. Beat eggs, sugar and salt together. Beat the flour into the mixture. Soften or just melt the butter, beat into the mixture with the lemon rind. Pour mixture round apples. Bake in a moderate oven, Mark 4, 350°F (180°C) for 40-45 minutes. Decorate with cherries and eat hot or cold.
If an ovenproof dish is not available this can be made in a cake tin and turned out of the tin to serve.

Couronne de pommes
Apple ring

For 6 servings:

- 1.5 kg (3 lb 4 oz) cooking apples
- 150 g (5 oz) sugar
- 1 teaspoon ground cinnamon
- 50 g (2 oz) butter
- 200 g (6 fl oz) double cream
- walnuts

Peel and roughly chop the apples. Generously butter a ring mould and fill with the apples, packing in well. Mix 100 g (3½ oz) of the sugar with 5 tablespoons water and add the ground cinnamon. Pour this mixture over the apples and dot with knobs of butter.
Cook in a moderate oven in a bain-marie for an hour. Turn out immediately and serve with cream whipped with the remaining sugar. Decorate with walnuts.

Pommes au four (1)
Baked apples

For 8 servings:

- 1.5 kg (3 lb 4 oz) cooking apples
- 100 g (3½ oz) caster sugar
- 100 g (3½ oz) raisins
- ½ glass rum
- 50 g (2 oz) butter

Peel and cut the apples into quarters. Butter an oven-proof dish and pack the apple pieces in well. Cover with the raisins soaked in rum, and finally top with small knobs of the remaining butter. Cook for an hour in a moderate oven and serve hot or warm.
These baked apples may be served with fresh cream.

Pommes au four (2)

Baked apples

For 6 servings:

- **6 cooking apples**
- **50 g (2 oz) butter**
- **100 g (3½ oz) quince jelly**
- **1 lemon**

Peel and core the apples and sprinkle with lemon juice. Place these apples in an ovenproof dish and top each with a knob of butter.
Bake in a moderate oven Mark 4, 350°F (180°C) for 45 minutes.
Half-way through baking, pour a little quince jelly over each apple.
Serve in the baking dish.

Mousse au chocolat

Chocolate mousse

For 6 servings:

- **300 g (11 oz) plain chocolate**
- **6 eggs**
- **200 g (7 oz) caster sugar**
- **1 orange**
- **salt**

Separate the yolks from the whites of the eggs. Work the sugar into the yolks and whisk the mixture until pale. Put the squares of chocolate into a saucepan and cover with water. Heat gently until the chocolate melts. Carefully draw off the water without disturbing the chocolate.
Stir the melted chocolate briskly into the egg yolks.
Whisk the egg whites into a snow, add a pinch of salt, and gently fold into the chocolate. Add a teaspoonful of grated orange rind to the mousse.
Keep in a cool place and serve well chilled.

Gâteau roulé aux fraises
Strawberry roll

For 8 servings:

– **250 g (9 oz) plain flour**
– **250 g (9 oz) caster sugar**
– **125 g (4½ oz) butter**
– **8 eggs**
– **pinch of salt**
– **500 g (1 lb 2 oz) strawberries**

Whisk the eggs and sugar briskly in a bowl over hot water. Gradually add the flour, melted butter, and finally a pinch of salt. Wash and hull the strawberries and dry well. Pour the mixture onto a large, well-buttered baking sheet and spread evenly.
Bake in a hot oven Mark 4, 350°F (180°C) and as soon as the edges begin to turn brown, remove from the oven.
Slide the 'sponge' onto a kitchen cloth, quickly spread with strawberries, and immediately roll up while hot. If you wait for too long, the 'sponge' becomes brittle. Decorate with strawberries and sprinkle with sugar.

Pain perdu
Bread pudding with rum and raisins

For 8 servings:

– **1 kg (2 lb 2 oz) stale bread**
– **1½ l (2½ pt) milk**
– **4 eggs**
– **3 dessertspoons oil**
– **100 g (3½ oz) raisins**
– **1 glass rum**
– **200 g (7 oz) caster sugar**
– **25 g (1 oz) butter**
– **1 dessertspoon ground cinnamon**
– **1 pinch salt**

Break the stale bread into large chunks and soak in the milk. Add the eggs, oil, ground cinnamon, sugar and the raisins, previously soaked in rum. Then add the rum and a pinch of salt. Mix together well. Butter an ovenproof dish and fill with this panada. Cook for 45 minutes in a hot oven, and serve hot or warm.

Tarte à la rhubarbe
Rhubarb tart

For 6 servings:

– **500 g (1 lb 2 oz) plain flour**
– **150 g (5 oz) butter**
– **1 egg**
– **pinch of salt**
– **1 kg (2 lb 2 oz) rhubarb**
– **150 g (5 oz) sugar**
– **double cream**
– **$\frac{1}{2}$ glass water**

Place the flour in a mixing bowl. Make a hole in the centre and add the egg, $\frac{1}{2}$ glass of water, a pinch of salt and the softened butter. Knead this pastry dough well, roll into a ball, and leave to rest.
Meanwhile, peel and cut the rhubarb into chunks. Put the rhubarb and sugar into a saucepan, and without adding water, cook on a low flame for an hour to evaporate the moisture.
Line a well-buttered flan ring with pastry and fill with rhubarb. With the remaining pastry, make a lattice on the tart.
Bake in a moderate oven Mark 4, 350°F (180°C).
Serve warm or cold with fresh cream.

Clafoutis aux cerises
Cherries baked in batter

For 8 servings:

– **1 kg (2 lb 2 oz) cherries**
– **150 g (5 oz) plain flour**
– **150 g (5 oz) sugar**
– **6 eggs**
– **150 g (4$\frac{1}{2}$ fl oz) double cream**
– **1 small glass kirsch**
– **butter**
– **salt**

Stone the cherries and arrange in a large buttered baking dish. Now blend the eggs with the sugar, gradually adding the flour, then the cream, kirsch, and a pinch of salt.
Pour this batter over the cherries and bake for about an hour in a moderate oven, Mark 4, 350°F (180°C).
Serve hot.

Suggested wines:

Petit Sauternes, Muscat de Frontignan

Gâteau au pamplemousse

Grapefruit cake

For 6 servings:

- 3 grapefruits
- 300 g (11 oz) caster sugar
- 4 eggs
- 250 g (9 oz) plain flour
- 150 g (5 oz) butter
- $\frac{1}{2}$ glass brandy
- 1$\frac{1}{2}$ teaspoon baking powder
- pinch of salt

Whisk together 200 g (7 oz) of the sugar with the eggs. Fold in the flour, melted butter and baking powder. Grate the zest of the grapefruits and add to the batter together with a pinch of salt.
Pour the mixture into a buttered cake tin.
Bake in a moderate oven, Mark 4, 350°F (180°C) for 45 minutes. When the cake is baked, leave until warm before turning out.
Peel and squeeze the juice from two of the grapefruits. Make a syrup using 50 g (2 oz) of the sugar, the brandy and this juice. Let the cake soak up this syrup.
Place some lump sugar and a little water on a high flame to make a pale caramel with which to glaze the cake. Decorate with peeled sections of the third grapefruit.

Gâteau marbré

Marble cake

For 6 servings:

- 250 g (10 oz) plain flour
- 300 g (11 oz) butter
- 300 g (11 oz) caster sugar
- 5 standard eggs
- 1 teaspoon baking powder
- 50 g (2 oz) chocolate powder

Cream together butter and sugar until light and fluffy. Beat in eggs in three stages. Divide this mixture in two halves. To one half add $\frac{1}{2}$ teaspoon baking powder and 150 g (6 oz) flour.
To the other half add remaining baking powder, 100 g (4 oz) flour and 2 oz chocolate powder.
Place alternate spoonfuls of mixture into a well greased 20 cm (8 in or 9 in) cake-tin.
Baking time 45 minutes approximately.
Once the cake has been turned out it may be covered with soft chocolate icing.

Tarte normande

Normandy apple tart

For 6 servings:

- 500 g (1 lb 2 oz) sweet flan pastry
- 1 kg (2 lb 2 oz) cooking apples
- 200 g (7 oz) almonds
- 1 dessertspoon ground cinnamon
- 50 g (2 oz) butter
- 100 g (3½ oz) caster sugar
- 25 g (1 oz) icing sugar

Prepare the sweet flan pastry and line a flan ring.
Bake in a moderate oven. Meanwhile, peel and cut apples into pieces. Cook slowly in a saucepan with the butter until the fruit is reduced to a thick pulp. Add the caster sugar. Fill the flan with this apple pulp.
Sprinkle first with chopped almonds, and then with a mixture of icing sugar and cinnamon.
Place under the grill for a few minutes and serve.

Tarte aux abricots et aux fraises

Apricot and strawberry flan

For 6 servings:

- 400 g (14 oz) short pastry
- 500 g (1 lb 2 oz) apricots
- 100 g (3½ oz) apricot jam
- 200 g (7 oz) strawberries

Line a flan ring with the pastry. Halve the apricots and arrange in the flan. Cook in a moderate oven for 45 minutes.
Remove from the oven and allow to cool. Melt the jam with a spoonful of water and pour over the flan. Cover with strawberries.

Fromage blanc aux pêches

Cream cheese with peaches

For 8 servings:

– **500 g (1 lb 4 oz) cream cheese**
– **150 g (4½ fl oz) double cream**
– **150 g (5 oz) caster sugar**
– **50 g (2 oz) raisins**
– **½ glass rum**
– **6 peaches**
– **hazelnuts**

Soak the raisins in the rum for two hours. Peel and quarter the peaches. Blend the cream cheese with the cream and sugar. Just before serving, fold the peaches and raisins into the cream cheese mixture. Sprinkle over with hazelnuts.
In winter, tinned peaches in syrup may be used.

Salade de fruits rouges

Red fruit salad

For 6 servings:

– **200 g (7 oz) redcurrants**
– **200 g (7 oz) raspberries**
– **400 g (14 oz) peaches**
– **100 g (3½ oz) sugar**
– **1 glass red wine preferably Burgundy**

Melt the sugar in the wine diluted with ½ l (1 pt) of water. Peel the fruit and place in a large fruit bowl. Pour the wine syrup over and leave to cool.
Serve well chilled.

Charlotte aux marrons
Chestnut charlotte

For 8 servings:

- 30 sponge fingers
- 4 egg yolks
- 50 g (2 oz) caster sugar
- 200 g (7 oz) butter
- 1 glass rum
- 1 kg (2 lb 2 oz) sweetened
  vanilla-flavoured chestnut purée
- 1.5 l (2½ pt) custard

Mix the yolks with the sugar and beat well. Soften the butter without melting, and blend into the eggs. Gradually add the chestnut purée. Mix well together and add the rum.

Line the base and sides of a charlotte mould with sponge fingers. Pour the chestnut purée into the prepared mould. Cover with the remaining sponge fingers. Keep in a cool place for a few hours.

Turn out just before serving and hand the custard as an accompaniment.

Charlotte aux pralines
Praline charlotte

For 6 servings:

- 24 sponge fingers
- 400 g (14 oz) chocolate
- 5 egg yolks
- 200 g (7 oz) caster sugar
- 150 g (5 oz) praline
- ½ glass of kirsch
- flaked almonds
- 1 pt custard

Line the base and sides of a charlotte mould with sponge fingers soaked in kirsch.

Melt the chocolate in a saucepan of water. When the chocolate is soft, remove from the saucepan without stirring. Cream the yolks with the sugar and add the chocolate. Fold the softened butter into the mixture with the grated praline. Fill the mould with this mixture.

Cover with a layer of sponge fingers and keep in a cool place.

Turn out just before serving and decorate with toasted, flaked almonds and praline. (Almonds covered with a coating of cooked sugar). Hand some custard as an accompaniment.

Recipe Index

Lobster à la normande, 92
Lobster breton, 92
Loin of lamb with herbs, 109

M

Mackerel in cream sauce, 84
Mackerel in white wine, 84
Mackerel with mustard, 85
Marble cake, 165
Marinated herrings, 85
Meat and cabbage soup, 39
Meat pie, 26
Mediterranean fisherman's soup, 40
Melon with ham, 30
Melted cheese with vegetables, 33
Milk soup, 49
Mulberry tart, 154
Mushroom tart, 70
Mushroom soufflé, 70
Mushroom soup, 46
Mussel soup, 43
Mussels with cream sauce, 88
Mussels with lemon, 86

N

Noodle soup, 38
Noodles, home-made, 21
Normandy apple tart, 166

O

Omelette provençal, 19
Onion flan, 29
Onion soup, 43
Oysters bordelaise, 90

P

Pancake gâteau with mushrooms, 28
Paprika veal, 104
Partridge with cabbage, 145
Partridge with sauerkraut, 145
Pâté in a pastry crust, 11
Peach and raspberry gâteau, 157
Pear flan, 156
Pears in their jackets, 156
Pears in wine, 155
Pepper salad, 124
Pepper steak, 98
Peppers provençal, 58
Pheasant with apples, 144
Pheasant with mushrooms and onions, 143
Pheasant with sauerkraut, 143
Pigeon with apples, 144
Pigeons with grapes, 137
Pike in cream sauce, 86
Potato ring, 66
Potatoes baked with milk, 60
Potted pork, 31
Praline charlotte, 168
Pumpkin soup, 42

R

Rabbit with dried haricot beans, 148
Rabbit with mustard, 147
Rabbit with olives, 148
Ragoût of wood pigeon, 146
Raw mushroom salad, 125
Red beans with bacon and sausages, 59
Red cabbage salad, 125
Red cabbage with apples, 54
Red cabbage with chestnuts and bacon, 59
Red cabbage with sausages, 63
Red fruit salad, 167
Red mullet with fennel, 79
Red mullet with tomatoes, 81

Rhubarb tart, 164
Rib steak with wine sauce, 99
Ring of sole, 78
Risotto, 64
Roquefort cheese canapés, 23

S

Saddle of venison, 149
Salad niçoise, 121
Salt cod in garlic mayonnaise, 83
Salt cod provençal, 83
Sarlat potatoes, 61
Sauerkraut garnished with bacon and sausages, 58
Sausage in a pastry crust, 31
Sauté chicken in curry sauce, 132
Sauté chicken with lemon, 136
Sauté potatoes with onions, 68
Sauté rabbit with bacon, 147
Savoury bread, 26
Scallops provençal, 77
Scallops with garlic, 77
Scrambled eggs, 19
Scrambled eggs with peppers, 17
Scrambled eggs with truffles, 14
Sea bream with fennel, 75
Shoulder of veal stuffed with eggs, 108
Skewered lamb, 111
Skewered mussels, 89
Smoked herrings in cream, 85
Smoked shoulder of pork with lentils, 112
Snails, 27
Snow eggs, 158
Soft-boiled egg, 33
Sorrel omelette, 18
Split pea purée with sausages, 56
Split pea soup, 46
Steak tartare, 101
Stewed knuckle of veal with lemon, 108
Stewed pears in caramel, 155
Stewed turnips, 60
Strawberry roll, 163
Stuffed aubergines, 65
Stuffed cabbage, 71
Stuffed figs, 154
Stuffed oysters, 90
Stuffed tomatoes with tuna, 16

T

Tomato flan, 55
Tomato soup, 45
Tomatoes with mushroom stuffing, 64
Tomatoes with pork stuffing, 65
Tournedos steaks with cream sauce, 103
Trout with almonds, 93
Turbot soup, 40
Turbot with hollandaise sauce, 81
Turkey stuffed with chestnuts, 135
Turnips baked with cream, 60

V

Veal escalopes in breadcrumbs, 105
Veal escalopes with cream sauce, 104
Veal olives, 105
Veal stew, 106
Veal stewed with wine and tomatoes, 106
Vegetable ring in aspic jelly, 69
Vegetable soup flavoured with basil, 37
Vegetable soup with barley, 42

W

Watercress soup, 49
White beans in cream sauce, 68
Wild duck with apples, 142
Wild duck with turnips, 142

Index

Introduction, 4

Contents, 5

Translation:
Michael and Pamela Hopf

Illustrations:
Christian Roland Délu

Jacket design:
David Roberts

Editorial co-ordination:
Beatrice Frei

*Grateful thanks for all the help in the preparation of this book
are given to:*

Carole McWhirter
Denise Cadisch
The Department of Catering, Southgate Technical College,
(E. R. Burman, Head of Department).

ISBN 0812060857

Printed by A.I.P., Argenteuil, France.